Psalms Simple Prayers

Devotional book 5

DONNA ROBINSON

DONNA ROBINSON

ISBN: 1537064606
ISBN-13: 978 1537064604

DONNA ROBINSON

DEDICATION
I dedicate this book to all who search to understand the knowledge of our Lord
and Savior Jesus Christ

DONNA ROBINSON

CONTENTS

DONNA ROBINSON

ACKNOWLEDGMENTS

I would like to acknowledge the Lord Jesus Christ for using me as a vessel of the Holy Spirit the wisdom to write, the motivation to mature, and the patience to progress.

INTRODUCTION

AS SAID IN BOOK 1, I WROTE THIS BOOK IN NEED OF UNDERSTANDING WHY DAVID WAS DESCRIBED AS "A MAN AFTER GOD'S HEART" (ACTS. 13:22 & 1 SAM. 13:14).

BOOK 5 IS THE CLOSING OF A NEW BEGINNING. A COMBINATION OF REJUVENATING MUSIC MIXED WITH HEARTFUL HALLELUJAHS CREATE A PRAISE THAT WILL NOT QUIT!

THE PURPOSE OF THIS DEVOTIONAL BOOK:

1. **STUDY** THE PSALM
2. **READ** THE REVEALTION
3. **RELEASE** PRAYER

DONNA ROBINSON

SHOW AND TELL

Psalm 107
1 Give thanks to the Lord, for he is good;
   his love endures forever.
2 Let the redeemed of the Lord tell their story
   those he redeemed from the hand of the foe,
3 those he gathered from the lands,
   from east and west, from north and south.
4 Some wandered in desert wastelands,
   finding no way to a city where they could settle.
5 They were hungry and thirsty,
   and their lives ebbed away.
6 Then they cried out to the Lord in their trouble,
   and he delivered them from their distress.
7 He led them by a straight way
   to a city where they could settle.
8 Let them give thanks to the Lord for his unfailing love
   and his wonderful deeds for mankind,
9 for he satisfies the thirsty
   and fills the hungry with good things.
10 Some sat in darkness, in utter darkness,
   prisoners suffering in iron chains,
11 because they rebelled against God's commands
   and despised the plans of the Most High.
12 So he subjected them to bitter labor;
   they stumbled, and there was no one to help.
13 Then they cried to the Lord in their trouble,
   and he saved them from their distress.
14 He brought them out of darkness, the utter darkness,
   and broke away their chains.
15 Let them give thanks to the Lord for his unfailing love
   and his wonderful deeds for mankind,
16 for he breaks down gates of bronze
   and cuts through bars of iron.
17 Some became fools through their rebellious ways
   and suffered affliction because of their iniquities.
18 They loathed all food
   and drew near the gates of death.
19 Then they cried to the Lord in their trouble,
   and he saved them from their distress.
20 He sent out his word and healed them;
   he rescued them from the grave.

21 Let them give thanks to the Lord for his unfailing love
   and his wonderful deeds for mankind.
22 Let them sacrifice thank offerings
   and tell of his works with songs of joy.
23 Some went out on the sea in ships;
   they were merchants on the mighty waters.
24 They saw the works of the Lord,
   his wonderful deeds in the deep.
25 For he spoke and stirred up a tempest
   that lifted high the waves.
26 They mounted up to the heavens and went down to the depths;
   in their peril their courage melted away.
27 They reeled and staggered like drunkards;
   they were at their wits' end.
28 Then they cried out to the Lord in their trouble,
   and he brought them out of their distress.
29 He stilled the storm to a whisper;
   the waves of the sea were hushed.
30 They were glad when it grew calm,
   and he guided them to their desired haven.
31 Let them give thanks to the Lord for his unfailing love
   and his wonderful deeds for mankind.
32 Let them exalt him in the assembly of the people
   and praise him in the council of the elders.
33 He turned rivers into a desert,
   flowing springs into thirsty ground,
34 and fruitful land into a salt waste,
   because of the wickedness of those who lived there.
35 He turned the desert into pools of water
   and the parched ground into flowing springs;
36 there he brought the hungry to live,
   and they founded a city where they could settle.
37 They sowed fields and planted vineyards
   that yielded a fruitful harvest;
38 he blessed them, and their numbers greatly increased,
   and he did not let their herds diminish.
39 Then their numbers decreased, and they were humbled
   by oppression, calamity and sorrow;
40 he who pours contempt on nobles
   made them wander in a trackless waste.
41 But he lifted the needy out of their affliction
   and increased their families like flocks.
42 The upright see and rejoice,
   but all the wicked shut their mouths.

43 Let the one who is wise heed these things
and ponder the loving deeds of the Lord.

This Psalm reminds us of the lasting love of God's works through five different complicated lifestyle dilemmas:

Vs.4-8: Lost souls, backsliders, broken hearts, and those who are weak in faith

Vs. 10-16: Prisoners who are sent away because of sin, rebellion acts, or bad behavior

Vs. 17-21: Those who are physically sick caused by sin or previous irresponsible actions

Vs. 23-32: Those out at sea (in those days much business was conducted out at sea) today's common language would be called those in the workplace

Vs. 35-42: Those who have encountered with wilderness situations turned into flourishing harvests

Five very different scenarios but identical outcomes displaying their need for God. Go forth and tell of His lasting love for all to take notice, follow, and obey.

PRAYER

I give thanks to the Lord for His lasting love towards me. This little light of mine I will let shine that men would glorify the Father (Matt. 5:16). Whoever comes to You, You will not reject them (John 6:37). You will love them and show them Your salvation. I thank You for saving me from every wilderness situation, every dark and deserted relationship, and all of my foolish habits and behaviors. I am so undeserving of Your redemption. I will show and tell of Your goodness that lead men to repentance (Rom. 2:4). I will show and tell of the gospel that profits me with wisdom and correction. I will show and tell to make disciples as You said in Your word he who wins souls is wise (Proverbs 11:30). I decrease so You may increase (John 3:30). In Jesus name I pray Amen.

HE GOT THIS

Psalm 108
A song. A psalm of David.

1 My heart, O God, is steadfast;
  I will sing and make music with all my soul.
2 Awake, harp and lyre!
  I will awaken the dawn.
3 I will praise you, Lord, among the nations;
  I will sing of you among the peoples.
4 For great is your love, higher than the heavens;
  your faithfulness reaches to the skies.
5 Be exalted, O God, above the heavens;
  let your glory be over all the earth.
6 Save us and help us with your right hand,
  that those you love may be delivered.
7 God has spoken from his sanctuary:
  "In triumph I will parcel out Shechem
  and measure off the Valley of Sukkoth.
8 Gilead is mine, Manasseh is mine;
  Ephraim is my helmet,
  Judah is my scepter.
9 Moab is my washbasin,
  on Edom I toss my sandal;
  over Philistia I shout in triumph."
10 Who will bring me to the fortified city?
  Who will lead me to Edom?
11 Is it not you, God, you who have rejected us
  and no longer go out with our armies?
12 Give us aid against the enemy,
  for human help is worthless.
13 With God we will gain the victory,
  and he will trample down our enemies.

Each of us has a capacity for God and an ability to relate to Him in a personal way. When we do He brings to us pardon for the past, peace for the present, and a promise for the future (Ralph Bell). This quote identifies with David's expectation in God alone.

His attitude was upright and not uptight in situations beyond his control. Battles are meant to make one stronger not weaker. The evidence of a steadfast or faithful heart in sync with His words gives the stability to move forward even when you cannot see what is ahead. David turned up his praise knowing the battle has already been won!

❖Psalm 57 7-11 & 60 5-12: Same words not exact different occasion could be a consistent prayer David prayed

PRAYER

Father I pray Your word in 2 Corinthians 4: 8-9… We are hard pressed on every side, but not crushed; perplexed, but not in despair; persecuted, but not abandoned; struck down, but not destroyed. I know You are for me although it may be many against me. I stand and shout **FATHER YOU GOT THIS**! Like David I will praise with the right attitude. What does not kill me makes me stronger! I say with confidence the Lord is my helper, I will not be afraid (Heb. 13:6). The Lord is my light and my salvation whom shall I fear; the Lord is the stronghold of my life of whom shall I be afraid (Psalm 27:1). For great is your love higher than the heavens; your faithfulness reaches towards the skies (vs.4). I look to Your direction to sing and make music with all my soul. As long as I walk with You I walk as a winner! In Jesus name I pray Amen.

DONNA ROBINSON

SET THE RECORD STRAIGHT

Psalm 109
For the director of music. Of David. A psalm.

1 My God, whom I praise,
  do not remain silent,
2 for people who are wicked and deceitful
  have opened their mouths against me;
  they have spoken against me with lying tongues.
3 With words of hatred they surround me;
  they attack me without cause.
4 In return for my friendship they accuse me,
  but I am a man of prayer.
5 They repay me evil for good,
  and hatred for my friendship.
6 Appoint someone evil to oppose my enemy;
  let an accuser stand at his right hand.
7 When he is tried, let him be found guilty,
  and may his prayers condemn him.
8 May his days be few;
  may another take his place of leadership.
9 May his children be fatherless
  and his wife a widow.
10 May his children be wandering beggars;
  may they be driven from their ruined homes.
11 May a creditor seize all he has;
  may strangers plunder the fruits of his labor.
12 May no one extend kindness to him
  or take pity on his fatherless children.
13 May his descendants be cut off,
  their names blotted out from the next generation.
14 May the iniquity of his fathers be remembered before the Lord;
  may the sin of his mother never be blotted out.
15 May their sins always remain before the Lord,
  that he may blot out their name from the earth.
16 For he never thought of doing a kindness,
  but hounded to death the poor
  and the needy and the brokenhearted.
17 He loved to pronounce a curse
  may it come back on him.
  He found no pleasure in blessing
  may it be far from him.

18 He wore cursing as his garment;
  it entered into his body like water,
  into his bones like oil.
19 May it be like a cloak wrapped about him,
  like a belt tied forever around him.
20 May this be the Lord's payment to my accusers,
  to those who speak evil of me.
21 But you, Sovereign Lord,
  help me for your name's sake;
  out of the goodness of your love, deliver me.
22 For I am poor and needy,
  and my heart is wounded within me.
23 I fade away like an evening shadow;
  I am shaken off like a locust.
24 My knees give way from fasting;
  my body is thin and gaunt.
25 I am an object of scorn to my accusers;
  when they see me, they shake their heads.
26 Help me, Lord my God;
  save me according to your unfailing love.
27 Let them know that it is your hand,
  that you, Lord, have done it.
28 While they curse, may you bless;
  may those who attack me be put to shame,
  but may your servant rejoice.
29 May my accusers be clothed with disgrace
  and wrapped in shame as in a cloak.
30 With my mouth I will greatly extol the Lord;
  in the great throng of worshipers I will praise him.
31 For he stands at the right hand of the needy,
  to save their lives from those who would condemn them.

When the going gets tough **PRAY**! When bad things happen to good people **PRAY**! When treated unfairly **PRAY**! When your heart is broken and fear is staring you right in your face **PRAY**! David's gutsy prayer of revenge against every enemy in his life proved him innocent in the eyes of God. Constantly being condemned, pressured with pain, and dealing with deceit provoked him to praise!

God sweetens outward pain with inward peace (Thomas Watson). David gave into prayer to rehabilitate his position as a leader and a child of God. He understood God's ways and did not cop an attitude when all odds were against him. Verse 4 is my favorite as an awesome reminder on how to resolve and fight issues not with physical abilities or material weapons, but spiritually on purpose which brings lasting results.

PRAYER

- God, whom I praise through every trial I pray!
- Through every accusation I pray!
- Through every rejection I pray for I am a woman/man of **PRAYER**!

It is a must that I understand Your ways and not just Your acts. You are my deliverer and my strength and out of the goodness of Your love I will never be put to shame. I set the record straight and I give into the blessings that will result from this as I possess an attitude of praise. I set the record straight and continue to serve and give my all every single day, and not give into the weaknesses of my flesh. My haters and accusers have put their mouth on me for the last time. I now open my mouth and extol my Lord and Savior and take my rightful place in the One who gives me life. In Him I live, move, and have my being (Acts 17:28). In Jesus name I pray Amen.

FATHER AND SON

Psalm 110
Of David. A psalm.

1 The Lord says to my lord:
  "Sit at my right hand
  until I make your enemies
  a footstool for your feet."
2 The Lord will extend your mighty scepter from Zion, saying,
  "Rule in the midst of your enemies!"
3 Your troops will be willing
  on your day of battle.
  Arrayed in holy splendor,
  your young men will come to you
  like dew from the morning's womb.
4 The Lord has sworn
  and will not change his mind:
  "You are a priest forever,
  in the order of Melchizedek."
5 The Lord is at your right hand;
  he will crush kings on the day of his wrath.
6 He will judge the nations, heaping up the dead
  and crushing the rulers of the whole earth.
7 He will drink from a brook along the way,
  and so he will lift his head high.

This Psalm symbolizes true relationship David had with God. Verse 1 is mentioned in the Gospels of Matthew 22:44, Mark 12:36, and Luke 20:42-43 as David speaking under the inspiration of the Spirit. What a privilege that was to David; God trusted him so much that He would show him the future promise of His Only Son. He allowed David to speak and visualize in the Spirit the authority His Son will carry.

God engraved in David's heart how His Son will follow His

instructions to a tee; and as a result upgraded Him the highest seat in heaven (at the right). Literally this Psalm declares how divinity (heaven) though humanity (Jesus) will be established on earth. I am sure David was consumed in awe of this wonderful plan of salvation, power, and authority put in place. Perfected in every way to the point it will never have to be done over again!

PRAYER

For God so loved the world that he gave his only begotten Son that whosoever shall believe in Him should have everlasting life (John 3:16). Today I want to honor the word that became flesh, full of grace and truth (John 1:14). If it had not been for the perfect love of a true Father giving me life through the death of His Son (Romans 5:8) I would be dead. Thank You for the perfect plan of salvation through Jesus Christ that positions me as a child of God. I understand I have many choices placed before me which will determine my destiny, therefore I must present my body as a living sacrifice daily (Romans 12:1). Jesus was obedient to the point of death (Phil. 2:8) this does not exclude me. I pray I remain obedient to You and not my flesh. I want the Holy Spirit to rule in me, live in me, guide me, and instruct me. I totally rely on Your word and have expectant hope in the scriptures (NIV Version):

John 5:1-2 & 11-12

1-2 reads: Everyone who believes that Jesus is the Christ is born of God, and everyone who loves the father loves his child as well. [2] This is how we know that we love the children of God: by loving God and carrying out his commands.

11-12 reads: And this is the testimony: God has given us eternal life, and this life is in his Son. [12] Whoever has the Son has life; whoever does not have the Son of God does not have life.

In Jesus name I pray Amen.

SATISFACTION GUARANTEED

Psalm 111

1 Praise the Lord.
  I will extol the Lord with all my heart
  in the council of the upright and in the assembly.
2 Great are the works of the Lord;
  they are pondered by all who delight in them.
3 Glorious and majestic are his deeds,
  and his righteousness endures forever.
4 He has caused his wonders to be remembered;
  the Lord is gracious and compassionate.
5 He provides food for those who fear him;
  he remembers his covenant forever.
6 He has shown his people the power of his works,
  giving them the lands of other nations.
7 The works of his hands are faithful and just;
  all his precepts are trustworthy.
8 They are established for ever and ever,
  enacted in faithfulness and uprightness.
9 He provided redemption for his people;
  he ordained his covenant forever
  holy and awesome is his name.
10 The fear of the Lord is the beginning of wisdom;
  all who follow his precepts have good understanding.
  To him belongs eternal praise.

The skillfulness and mastery of God's creation and His works cannot be compared to man's expertise. No one respects a copycat, the original will always outlast its' competitors. This Psalm simply put in thorough detail sums of God's quality seal of approval promise. Every work, word, and purpose of His power yesterday, today, and eternal. I will (vs.1) positions the reader in action to remember God's principles and standards as a believer.

Taking God at His word provides an amazing opportunity to learn and mature in the character of His principles. This type of work cannot be duplicated, revoked, violated, fail, or disappoint. This work has a lifetime guarantee and will never break, weaken, die, or fade.

PRAYER

Great are the works of the Lord; they are pondered by all who delight in them (vs.2). The fear of the Lord is the beginning of wisdom; all who follow his precepts have good understanding (vs.10). I praise as You satisfy me with long life. I delight in understanding Your ways that mature me through my journey. I thank You that I know my life is settled in righteousness. I will remember Your word when tests of life push me to give up. I will pass every test as You have provided redemption for me to prosper! Hallelujah all praise and glory belongs to You God.

Mighty are the works of Your hands

Perfect are all of Your ways

Everlasting are your hands of strength

Faithful is Your unconditional love

All sufficient is Your grace

Great are you Lord; in all the earth in Jesus name I pray Amen.

UPRIGHT NOT UPTIGHT

Psalm 112

1 Praise the Lord.
  Blessed are those who fear the Lord,
  who find great delight in his commands.
2 Their children will be mighty in the land;
  the generation of the upright will be blessed.
3 Wealth and riches are in their houses,
  and their righteousness endures forever.
4 Even in darkness light dawns for the upright,
  for those who are gracious and compassionate and righteous.
5 Good will come to those who are generous and lend freely,
  who conduct their affairs with justice.
6 Surely the righteous will never be shaken;
  they will be remembered forever.
7 They will have no fear of bad news;
  their hearts are steadfast, trusting in the Lord.
8 Their hearts are secure, they will have no fear;
  in the end they will look in triumph on their foes.
9 They have freely scattered their gifts to the poor,
  their righteousness endures forever;
  their horn[m] will be lifted high in honor.
10 The wicked will see and be vexed,
  they will gnash their teeth and waste away;
  the longings of the wicked will come to nothing.

The first step towards getting somewhere is to decide that you are not going to stay where you are (John Pierpont Morgan). This Psalm summarizes the blessings of life that come to those who follow the instructions of God. No one is excluded from obtaining this justification of assured promises of a setup to win in life. It is not easy to walk upright. Life is usually an obstacle course of blood, sweat, and tears. Most times it is easier to walk uptight and "belong" rather than taking the high road and doing the right thing!

This Psalm is a secure promise even in our stumbles we have the stability to stand and pull through. No one or thing can strip you of this strength unless it is given permission to. An upright believer is strongest when weakness is given over to God and continue to move forward. When life gives you lemons, pitch a tent of obedience in God's word and make lemonade!

PRAYER

Lord forgive me for being uptight, pressured, and angry when life throws curveballs. I realize pain is always indication of purpose pushing me forward. Help me to mature in righteous living, mindset, and behaviors. I honor and respect Your word that all things are working for my good (Rom. 8:28). Getting upset, arguing, and not getting **"MY"** way creates negative results and adds nothing to my life. My connections and atmospheres are critical to my spiritual growth. I will be careful to make better decisions in these areas to walk upright. My steps are ordered (Psalm 37:23) and I declare Your word in Proverbs 23:18… There is surely a future hope for you and your hope will not be cut off. Holy Spirit teach me, word of God inspire me, and hope of God encourage me. In Jesus name I pray Amen.

A CALL TO PRAISE

Psalm 113

1 Praise the Lord.
  Praise the Lord, you his servants;
  praise the name of the Lord.
2 Let the name of the Lord be praised,
  both now and forevermore.
3 From the rising of the sun to the place where it sets,
  the name of the Lord is to be praised.
4 The Lord is exalted over all the nations,
  his glory above the heavens.
5 Who is like the Lord our God,
  the One who sits enthroned on high,
6 who stoops down to look
  on the heavens and the earth?
7 He raises the poor from the dust
  and lifts the needy from the ash heap;
8 he seats them with princes,
  with the princes of his people.
9 He settles the childless woman in her home
  as a happy mother of children.
  Praise the Lord.

Who can be humbled and lifted high at the same time? Who can raise and lift at the same time? Who can carry burdens and strength at the same time? This Psalm pleases the reader to praise the Lord not only for what He has done but for **WHO HE IS**! His name shall be praised. Not even the light of day nor the darkness of night can outlast the praise of His name. God is so concerned about praise it captures His attention! Let all who live learn to praise His name! Let all who are broken and barren find joy in His name! Let all who are weak and needy gain power through His name! Let all who serve Him praise His name!

PRAYER

Praise the Lord! I will give praise to Your name for You are worthy. The Lord is my strength and my song he has become my salvation. He is my God, and I will praise Him (Exodus 15:2). I will give praise to Your name for You have been more than good to me. I will continually offer a sacrifice of praise from the fruit of my lips that confess your name (Heb. 13:15). I will praise when times are good, bad, dark, light, broken and blessed. From the rising of the sun to the going down of the same the name of the Lord is to be praised (vs.3). In Jesus name I praise and pray Amen.

EARTH QUAKES

Psalm 114

1 When Israel came out of Egypt,
  Jacob from a people of foreign tongue,
2 Judah became God's sanctuary,
  Israel his dominion.
3 The sea looked and fled,
  the Jordan turned back;
4 the mountains leaped like rams,
  the hills like lambs.
5 Why was it, sea, that you fled?
  Why, Jordan, did you turn back?
6 Why, mountains, did you leap like rams,
  you hills, like lambs?
7 Tremble, earth, at the presence of the Lord,
  at the presence of the God of Jacob,
8 who turned the rock into a pool,
  the hard rock into springs of water.

The deliverance of the Israelites out of Egypt will never be forgotten. The transition to the promised land is a timeless breakthrough spoken of to this very day. These two stories of triumphant victory credit all the praise to God. God really loved His people; He did not like to see them pout and give up on what He had purpose for them. At the very presence of His Glory He held back every type of nature known to man move out of the way; and make way for His people to succeed in purpose.

This Psalm poses a question "Why did nature respond as it did fleeing and trembling?; .... the answer is only found in the very essence of God's power and His insistent authority not only in heaven but on earth as well. This Psalm comforts in assuring that God is in control.

PRAYER

Genesis 1:1 says… In the beginning God created the heavens and the earth. Everything You spoke to be became. Everything You spoke to existence expanded. Everything You spoke in power You purposed. Every word You declared in the spirit submits to Your authority. Even as You made a way for the people of Egypt I know You have made a way for me. Release Your glory in the earth to restore me. Dry up the deep waters of life that persist to drown me and deliver me from them. Let every mountain that attempts to blind me break into pieces that lead me to breakthrough! The earth is the Lord's and everything in it (Psalm 24:1 & 1 Corinthians 10:26). The whole earth quakes at Your power. Your name shakes the seas. Your presence fills me with Living Water. I praise You all the days of my life, You are in control in Jesus name I pray Amen.

DONNA ROBINSON

ALL GLORY NO GIMMICKS

Psalm 115

1 Not to us, Lord, not to us
   but to your name be the glory,
   because of your love and faithfulness.
2 Why do the nations say,
   "Where is their God?"
3 Our God is in heaven;
   he does whatever pleases him.
4 But their idols are silver and gold,
   made by human hands.
5 They have mouths, but cannot speak,
   eyes, but cannot see.
6 They have ears, but cannot hear,
   noses, but cannot smell.
7 They have hands, but cannot feel,
   feet, but cannot walk,
   nor can they utter a sound with their throats.
8 Those who make them will be like them,
   and so will all who trust in them.
9 All you Israelites, trust in the Lord
   he is their help and shield.
10 House of Aaron, trust in the Lord
   he is their help and shield.
11 You who fear him, trust in the Lord
   he is their help and shield.
12 The Lord remembers us and will bless us:
   He will bless his people Israel,
   he will bless the house of Aaron,
13 he will bless those who fear the Lord
   small and great alike.
14 May the Lord cause you to flourish,
   both you and your children.
15 May you be blessed by the Lord,
   the Maker of heaven and earth.
16 The highest heavens belong to the Lord,
   but the earth he has given to mankind.
17 It is not the dead who praise the Lord,
   those who go down to the place of silence;
18 it is we who extol the Lord,
   both now and forevermore.
   Praise the Lord.

Many times in life the flashy, fast, and free choices are not all meant to fit our purpose. Decisions we make today dictate our tomorrow. This Psalm makes a clear distinction between those who love God and those who lust after other gods. A prayer of despair to trust and remember the Lord in all of the decisions in life speaks to the Israelites. A promise of increase and blessings are given to those and generations thereafter who give into the glory of God and not the gimmicks of man.

PRAYER

Not to us, O Lord, not to us but to your name be the glory because of your love and faithfulness (vs.1). Every day I am changed into Your image with ever increasing glory (2 Corinthians 3:18). My heart is Your home. Let Your glory revealed through me to lead others to You. I will not allow negative images or idols strip me of my increase. May the Lord make you increase both you and your children. May you be blessed by the Lord the maker of heaven and earth (vs.14-15) in Jesus name I pray Amen.

DONNA ROBINSON

CALL ON HIS NAME

Psalm 116
1 I love the Lord, for he heard my voice;
  he heard my cry for mercy.
2 Because he turned his ear to me,
  I will call on him as long as I live.
3 The cords of death entangled me,
  the anguish of the grave came over me;
  I was overcome by distress and sorrow.
4 Then I called on the name of the Lord:
  "Lord, save me!"
5 The Lord is gracious and righteous;
  our God is full of compassion.
6 The Lord protects the unwary;
  when I was brought low, he saved me.
7 Return to your rest, my soul,
  for the Lord has been good to you.
8 For you, Lord, have delivered me from death,
  my eyes from tears,
  my feet from stumbling,
9 that I may walk before the Lord
  in the land of the living.
10 I trusted in the Lord when I said,
  "I am greatly afflicted";
11 in my alarm I said,
  "Everyone is a liar."
12 What shall I return to the Lord
  for all his goodness to me?
13 I will lift up the cup of salvation
  and call on the name of the Lord.
14 I will fulfill my vows to the Lord
  in the presence of all his people.
15 Precious in the sight of the Lord
  is the death of his faithful servants.
16 Truly I am your servant, Lord;
  I serve you just as my mother did;
  you have freed me from my chains.
17 I will sacrifice a thank offering to you
  and call on the name of the Lord.
18 I will fulfill my vows to the Lord
  in the presence of all his people,
19 in the courts of the house of the Lord

in your midst, Jerusalem.
Praise the Lord.

This Psalm takes place during a chaotic point in life but still brings comfort at the same time. Half past dead and drowned by the turn of events blocking breakthrough; God is eager to provide relief. The psalmist did not hold back the truth in finding complete peace in calling upon the name of the Lord. Unashamed and doing whatever it takes to please the Lord released fear, guilt, grief, disorder, and the opinion of man from life. God does not need a physical death but a spiritual death. This lifestyle remains committed to serving, believing, holy living, and intimacy and this is what He values. Values instilled in the life of every believer build solidity in God's word. Immediate offerings of thanks and praise, verses complaining and remaining were heard. The mercies of God take flight to rescue the cries of those who call on His name.

Call out the many names of God in your prayers today:

Creator of heaven and earth	Light of the world
Jehovah	Lion and the Lamb
Alpha and Omega	My resting place
Provider	Lily in the valley
Restorer and Redeemer	Balm of Gilead
True vine	Messiah
Yahweh	The Great I Am
Prince of Peace	Strong tower
Jehovah Sabaoth (Lord of Host)	Deliverer
Voice of Truth	El Shaddai
The second Adam	Defender

Maker of Salvation	Tried and True
Savior	The Anointed One
Hosanna in the Highest	Source of strength
Sanctifier	Chief Cornerstone
Solid Rock	Very present help
Faithful	Maker of glory
Omniscient	Omnipotent
King of Kings	Lifter of my head
Healer	Mender of broken hearts
The great Physician	Keeper
Way maker	The Way, The Truth, and The Life

I have complete hope in the assurance of Your great name and I call on You in Jesus name I pray Amen.

A PRAISE TO LOVE

Psalm 117

1 Praise the Lord, all you nations;
  extol him, all you peoples.
2 For great is his love toward us,
  and the faithfulness of the Lord endures forever.
  Praise the Lord.

The shortest Psalm in the book with rich content speaks volumes. Nations and people of **ALL** kind have the opportunity to experience and encounter God's love. The nature of God's love is so pure, tremendously forgiving, unending, and always ready to be put to use for whosoever will receive it. This is not a cupid puppy love that flutters and goes away. This love is sure to be a pit-bull unshakable bond that will touch the hardest heart. A praise response is necessary to seize this undeserving gift of love. This love gives every believer permission to be loved even when no one else does! Praise the Lord!

PRAYER

Pray Psalms 117 (and speak this prayer) ... I praise You for Your loving-kindness is better than life. What a privilege it is that You don't treat us as our sins deserve (Psalm 103:10). You sing over us and quiet us with Your love (Zep. 3:17). Oh Lord your love lifts me higher and gives me strength to go on. I submit to Your love for me that breaks me free from all the shackles of life. Reduce me to love where I have been hurt, wounded, and abused. Love will be the anchor that guides me into the deep truths of Your word. I praise Your name for Your agape love in Jesus name I pray Amen.

DONNA ROBINSON

REPEATED RECEPIENT OF GOD'S LOVE

Psalm 118

1 Give thanks to the Lord, for he is good;
  his love endures forever.
2 Let Israel say:
  "His love endures forever."
3 Let the house of Aaron say:
  "His love endures forever."
4 Let those who fear the Lord say:
  "His love endures forever."
5 When hard pressed, I cried to the Lord;
  he brought me into a spacious place.
6 The Lord is with me; I will not be afraid.
  What can mere mortals do to me?
7 The Lord is with me; he is my helper.
  I look in triumph on my enemies.
8 It is better to take refuge in the Lord
  than to trust in humans.
9 It is better to take refuge in the Lord
  than to trust in princes.
10 All the nations surrounded me,
  but in the name of the Lord I cut them down.
11 They surrounded me on every side,
  but in the name of the Lord I cut them down.
12 They swarmed around me like bees,
  but they were consumed as quickly as burning thorns;
  in the name of the Lord I cut them down.
13 I was pushed back and about to fall,
  but the Lord helped me.
14 The Lord is my strength and my defense;
  he has become my salvation.
15 Shouts of joy and victory
  resound in the tents of the righteous:
  "The Lord's right hand has done mighty things!
16   The Lord's right hand is lifted high;
  the Lord's right hand has done mighty things!"
17 I will not die but live,
  and will proclaim what the Lord has done.
18 The Lord has chastened me severely,
  but he has not given me over to death.

19 Open for me the gates of the righteous;
   I will enter and give thanks to the Lord.
20 This is the gate of the Lord
   through which the righteous may enter.
21 I will give you thanks, for you answered me;
   you have become my salvation.
22 The stone the builders rejected
   has become the cornerstone;
23 the Lord has done this,
   and it is marvelous in our eyes.
24 The Lord has done it this very day;
   let us rejoice today and be glad.
25 Lord, save us!
   Lord, grant us success!
26 Blessed is he who comes in the name of the Lord.
   From the house of the Lord we bless you.
27 The Lord is God,
   and he has made his light shine on us.
   With boughs in hand, join in the festal procession
   up to the horns of the altar.
28 You are my God, and I will praise you;
   you are my God, and I will exalt you.
29 Give thanks to the Lord, for he is good;
   his love endures forever.

This Psalm is so refreshing as a reminder that there is no favoritism in His love. Repeatedly David is seen weeping from the unfair dealings of life. He counteracts them by pulling on the strength of his personal testimonies of victory through the righteousness of God. David's life became better when he learned from his mistakes and used them as a testimony to mature spiritually.

Much can be said of this rich Psalm as Christ is seen in a vision as a continuance model of a Father's love to all who take refuge in Him. The generations of yesterday and the future celebrate the authority and power of His enduring love. Not all will or have agreed with this plan for all mankind (vs.22) (also mentioned in Acts 4:11 & 1 Peter 2:7). As for those who do will take full delight in Him through the roughs and reliefs in life. The love of God allows the vision of His kingdom to shine throughout the earth and those who possess it. Give thanks to the Lord for He is good His love endures forever.

PRAYER

Give thanks to the Lord for he is good his love endures forever (vs.29). This is the day the Lord has made I will rejoice and be glad in it (vs.24). No one can separate me from Your love (Romans 8:39). No one can measure up to Your love (Ephesians 3:18). Mature me in Your love as I break free from artificial people who I expected would love me for me. This love You have for me makes me complete, confident, and comforted. I thank God for Jesus Christ who modeled the perfect plan so we can all have a standard to look up to. Push me to echo your love in my home, my job, my community, and in the marketplace. Your love sets me free from my past and blesses me forward to a favorable future. You are my God and I will give You thanks. You are my God and I will exalt You. Give thanks to the Lord for he is good his love endures forever (vs.28-29) in Jesus name I pray Amen.

INSTRUCTIONS WITHOUT EXCUSE

This Psalm is spoken with deep wisdom and written from true life experiences. It serves as a reminder to all generations from the average way of life to accelerated Kingdom living.

Some basic information about Psalms 119:

- Longest chapter in the Bible
- The Hebrew alphabet is displayed as a guide throughout the chapters
- Each alphabet contains eight versus each
- Authors of this Psalm are mainly linked to David

So much can be said of this incredible Psalm. Attempting to unpack it all would be an understatement. Thorough study of this Psalm benefits the reader to understand how to grow in the instructions of God. It strategically shapens the strong and withers the weak. Every eight versus teaches standards and principles that should be followed in order to prosper in how to live life as a Christian.

- Importance of instruction words mentioned several times (NIV version & M.W definitions):
    - Precepts: mentioned 21 times, a rule intended to regulate thoughts and behaviors
    - Decrees: mentioned 21 times, an order issued by a legal authority
    - Law: mentioned 45 times, rules recognized and imposed
    - Statues: mentioned 23 times / ruling or written law

Psalm 119
א Aleph

1 Blessed are those whose ways are blameless,
 who walk according to the law of the Lord.
2 Blessed are those who keep his statutes
 and seek him with all their heart
3 they do no wrong
 but follow his ways.
4 You have laid down precepts
 that are to be fully obeyed.
5 Oh, that my ways were steadfast
 in obeying your decrees!
6 Then I would not be put to shame
 when I consider all your commands.
7 I will praise you with an upright heart
 as I learn your righteous laws.
8 I will obey your decrees;
 do not utterly forsake me.

- **Verses 1-8: follow instructions + obey = blessed**

ב Beth

9 How can a young person stay on the path of purity?
 By living according to your word.
10 I seek you with all my heart;
 do not let me stray from your commands.
11 I have hidden your word in my heart
 that I might not sin against you.
12 Praise be to you, Lord;
 teach me your decrees.
13 With my lips I recount
 all the laws that come from your mouth.
14 I rejoice in following your statutes
 as one rejoices in great riches.
15 I meditate on your precepts
 and consider your ways.
16 I delight in your decrees;
 I will not neglect your word.

- **Verses 9-16: Study continually in the word, have a joy about this new life of salvation, do life in and on purpose**

ג Gimel

17 Be good to your servant while I live,
   that I may obey your word.
18 Open my eyes that I may see
   wonderful things in your law.
19 I am a stranger on earth;
   do not hide your commands from me.
20 My soul is consumed with longing
   for your laws at all times.
21 You rebuke the arrogant, who are accursed,
   those who stray from your commands.
22 Remove from me their scorn and contempt,
   for I keep your statutes.
23 Though rulers sit together and slander me,
   your servant will meditate on your decrees.
24 Your statutes are my delight;
   they are my counselors.

- **Verses 17-24: allow your life to be shaped and molded through the counsel of the word, let go and let God have His way**

ד Daleth

25 I am laid low in the dust;
   preserve my life according to your word.
26 I gave an account of my ways and you answered me;
   teach me your decrees.
27 Cause me to understand the way of your precepts,
   that I may meditate on your wonderful deeds.
28 My soul is weary with sorrow;
   strengthen me according to your word.
29 Keep me from deceitful ways;
   be gracious to me and teach me your law.
30 I have chosen the way of faithfulness;
   I have set my heart on your laws.
31 I hold fast to your statutes, Lord;
   do not let me be put to shame.
32 I run in the path of your commands,
   for you have broadened my understanding.

- **Verses 25-32: mistakes will not disqualify you from the promises of His word, you must submit**

ה He

33 Teach me, Lord, the way of your decrees,
   that I may follow it to the end.
34 Give me understanding, so that I may keep your law
   and obey it with all my heart.
35 Direct me in the path of your commands,
   for there I find delight.
36 Turn my heart toward your statutes
   and not toward selfish gain.
37 Turn my eyes away from worthless things;
   preserve my life according to your word.
38 Fulfill your promise to your servant,
   so that you may be feared.
39 Take away the disgrace I dread,
   for your laws are good.
40 How I long for your precepts!
   In your righteousness preserve my life.

- **Versus 33-40: be a God chaser not a people pleaser**

ו Waw

41 May your unfailing love come to me, Lord,
   your salvation, according to your promise;
42 then I can answer anyone who taunts me,
   for I trust in your word.
43 Never take your word of truth from my mouth,
   for I have put my hope in your laws.
44 I will always obey your law,
   for ever and ever.
45 I will walk about in freedom,
   for I have sought out your precepts.
46 I will speak of your statutes before kings
   and will not be put to shame,
47 for I delight in your commands
   because I love them.
48 I reach out for your commands, which I love,
   that I may meditate on your decrees.

- **Versus 41-48: learn how to keep your mouth shut and be a disciple through disruption, only speak what the word says about the situation**

ז Zayin

49 Remember your word to your servant,
   for you have given me hope.
50 My comfort in my suffering is this:
   Your promise preserves my life.
51 The arrogant mock me unmercifully,
   but I do not turn from your law.
52 I remember, Lord, your ancient laws,
   and I find comfort in them.
53 Indignation grips me because of the wicked,
   who have forsaken your law.
54 Your decrees are the theme of my song
   wherever I lodge.
55 In the night, Lord, I remember your name,
   that I may keep your law.
56 This has been my practice:
   I obey your precepts.

- **Versus 49-56: light will always outshine the dark, all problems have an expiration date, hold tight and find comfort in the word**

ח Heth

57 You are my portion, Lord;
   I have promised to obey your words.
58 I have sought your face with all my heart;
   be gracious to me according to your promise.
59 I have considered my ways
   and have turned my steps to your statutes.
60 I will hasten and not delay
   to obey your commands.
61 Though the wicked bind me with ropes,
   I will not forget your law.
62 At midnight I rise to give you thanks
   for your righteous laws.
63 I am a friend to all who fear you,

to all who follow your precepts.
64 The earth is filled with your love, Lord;
   teach me your decrees.

- **Versus 57-64: do not procrastinate or hesitate order, be determined and walk confident in the word**

ט Teth

65 Do good to your servant
   according to your word, Lord.
66 Teach me knowledge and good judgment,
   for I trust your commands.
67 Before I was afflicted I went astray,
   but now I obey your word.
68 You are good, and what you do is good;
   teach me your decrees.
69 Though the arrogant have smeared me with lies,
   I keep your precepts with all my heart.
70 Their hearts are callous and unfeeling,
   but I delight in your law.
71 It was good for me to be afflicted
   so that I might learn your decrees.
72 The law from your mouth is more precious to me
   than thousands of pieces of silver and gold.

- **Versus 65-72: do not reject constructive criticism and learn from your pain, be a good steward of God's word**

י Yodh

73 Your hands made me and formed me;
   give me understanding to learn your commands.
74 May those who fear you rejoice when they see me,
   for I have put my hope in your word.
75 I know, Lord, that your laws are righteous,
   and that in faithfulness you have afflicted me.
76 May your unfailing love be my comfort,
   according to your promise to your servant.
77 Let your compassion come to me that I may live,
   for your law is my delight.
78 May the arrogant be put to shame for wronging me without cause;
   but I will meditate on your precepts.
79 May those who fear you turn to me,

those who understand your statutes.
80 May I wholeheartedly follow your decrees,
    that I may not be put to shame.

•   Versus 73-80: allow the Potter's hand to shape you, form you, and build you to be an example

כ Kaph

81 My soul faints with longing for your salvation,
    but I have put my hope in your word.
82 My eyes fail, looking for your promise;
    I say, "When will you comfort me?"
83 Though I am like a wineskin in the smoke,
    I do not forget your decrees.
84 How long must your servant wait?
    When will you punish my persecutors?
85 The arrogant dig pits to trap me,
    contrary to your law.
86 All your commands are trustworthy;
    help me, for I am being persecuted without cause.
87 They almost wiped me from the earth,
    but I have not forsaken your precepts.
88 In your unfailing love preserve my life,
    that I may obey the statutes of your mouth.

•   Versus 81-88: you must have tough skin and maturity in God, do not let flesh rule; there is no quit in the word

ל Lamedh

89 Your word, Lord, is eternal;
    it stands firm in the heavens.
90 Your faithfulness continues through all generations;
    you established the earth, and it endures.
91 Your laws endure to this day,
    for all things serve you.
92 If your law had not been my delight,
    I would have perished in my affliction.
93 I will never forget your precepts,
    for by them you have preserved my life.
94 Save me, for I am yours;
    I have sought out your precepts.
95 The wicked are waiting to destroy me,

but I will ponder your statutes.
96 To all perfection I see a limit,
    but your commands are boundless.

- **Versus 89-96: The Lord establishes endless promises through the word**

מ Mem

97 Oh, how I love your law!
    I meditate on it all day long.
98 Your commands are always with me
    and make me wiser than my enemies.
99 I have more insight than all my teachers,
    for I meditate on your statutes.
100 I have more understanding than the elders,
    for I obey your precepts.
101 I have kept my feet from every evil path
    so that I might obey your word.
102 I have not departed from your laws,
    for you yourself have taught me.
103 How sweet are your words to my taste,
    sweeter than honey to my mouth!
104 I gain understanding from your precepts;
    therefore I hate every wrong path.

- **Versus 97-104: revelation comes by meditating and understanding the word, wisdom from the word guides you**

נ Nun

105 Your word is a lamp for my feet,
    a light on my path.
106 I have taken an oath and confirmed it,
    that I will follow your righteous laws.
107 I have suffered much;
    preserve my life, Lord, according to your word.
108 Accept, Lord, the willing praise of my mouth,
    and teach me your laws.
109 Though I constantly take my life in my hands,
    I will not forget your law.

110 The wicked have set a snare for me,
　　but I have not strayed from your precepts.
111 Your statutes are my heritage forever;
　　they are the joy of my heart.
112 My heart is set on keeping your decrees
　　to the very end

• **Versus 105-112: stay focused, keep your heart set on the word**

ס Samekh

113 I hate double-minded people,
　　but I love your law.
114 You are my refuge and my shield;
　　I have put my hope in your word.
115 Away from me, you evildoers,
　　that I may keep the commands of my God!
116 Sustain me, my God, according to your promise, and I will live;
　　do not let my hopes be dashed.
117 Uphold me, and I will be delivered;
　　I will always have regard for your decrees.
118 You reject all who stray from your decrees,
　　for their delusions come to nothing.
119 All the wicked of the earth you discard like dross;
　　therefore I love your statutes.
120 My flesh trembles in fear of you;
　　I stand in awe of your laws

• **Versus 113-120: set yourself apart from the average, comfortable, familiar, and the past**

ע Ayin

121 I have done what is righteous and just;
　　do not leave me to my oppressors.
122 Ensure your servant's well-being;
　　do not let the arrogant oppress me.
123 My eyes fail, looking for your salvation,
　　looking for your righteous promise.
124 Deal with your servant according to your love
　　and teach me your decrees.
125 I am your servant; give me discernment
　　that I may understand your statutes.

126 It is time for you to act, Lord;
   your law is being broken.
127 Because I love your commands
   more than gold, more than pure gold,
128 and because I consider all your precepts right,
   I hate every wrong path.

- **Versus 121-128: walk in righteousness and the Lord will deal with you and what is beyond your control**

פ Pe

129 Your statutes are wonderful;
   therefore I obey them.
130 The unfolding of your words gives light;
   it gives understanding to the simple.
131 I open my mouth and pant,
   longing for your commands.
132 Turn to me and have mercy on me,
   as you always do to those who love your name.
133 Direct my footsteps according to your word;
   let no sin rule over me.
134 Redeem me from human oppression,
   that I may obey your precepts.
135 Make your face shine on your servant
   and teach me your decrees.
136 Streams of tears flow from my eyes,
   for your law is not obeyed.

- **Versus 129-136: continue and journey through the word as a daily lifestyle and you will mature**

צ Tsadhe

137 You are righteous, Lord,
   and your laws are right.
138 The statutes you have laid down are righteous;
   they are fully trustworthy.
139 My zeal wears me out,
   for my enemies ignore your words.
140 Your promises have been thoroughly tested,
   and your servant loves them.
141 Though I am lowly and despised,

I do not forget your precepts.
142 Your righteousness is everlasting
and your law is true.
143 Trouble and distress have come upon me,
but your commands give me delight.
144 Your statutes are always righteous;
give me understanding that I may live.

• **Versus 137-144: make eternal decisions despite your surroundings**

ק Qoph

145 I call with all my heart; answer me, Lord,
and I will obey your decrees.
146 I call out to you; save me
and I will keep your statutes.
147 I rise before dawn and cry for help;
I have put my hope in your word.
148 My eyes stay open through the watches of the night,
that I may meditate on your promises.
149 Hear my voice in accordance with your love;
preserve my life, Lord, according to your laws.
150 Those who devise wicked schemes are near,
but they are far from your law.
151 Yet you are near, Lord,
and all your commands are true.
152 Long ago I learned from your statutes
that you established them to last forever.

• **Versus 145-152: call out to the Lord through the word and it will not fail you**

ר Resh

153 Look on my suffering and deliver me,
for I have not forgotten your law.
154 Defend my cause and redeem me;
preserve my life according to your promise.
155 Salvation is far from the wicked,
for they do not seek out your decrees.
156 Your compassion, Lord, is great;
preserve my life according to your laws.

157 Many are the foes who persecute me,
    but I have not turned from your statutes.
158 I look on the faithless with loathing,
    for they do not obey your word.
159 See how I love your precepts;
    preserve my life, Lord, in accordance with your love.
160 All your words are true;
    all your righteous laws are eternal.

- **Versus 153-160: God's word will fight for you, preserve you, defend you, and deliver you**

ש Sin and Shin

161 Rulers persecute me without cause,
    but my heart trembles at your word.
162 I rejoice in your promise
    like one who finds great spoil.
163 I hate and detest falsehood
    but I love your law.
164 Seven times a day I praise you
    for your righteous laws.
165 Great peace have those who love your law,
    and nothing can make them stumble.
166 I wait for your salvation, Lord,
    and I follow your commands.
167 I obey your statutes,
    for I love them greatly.
168 I obey your precepts and your statutes,
    for all my ways are known to you.

- **Versus 161-168: Love the commands by obeying them**

ת Taw

169 May my cry come before you, Lord;
    give me understanding according to your word.
170 May my supplication come before you;
    deliver me according to your promise.
171 May my lips overflow with praise,
    for you teach me your decrees.
172 May my tongue sing of your word,
    for all your commands are righteous.

173 May your hand be ready to help me,
    for I have chosen your precepts.
174 I long for your salvation, Lord,
    and your law gives me delight.
175 Let me live that I may praise you,
    and may your laws sustain me.
176 I have strayed like a lost sheep.
    Seek your servant,
        for I have not forgotten your commands.

- **Versus 169-176: follow the leading of His word**

PRAYER

Continue to meditate on Psalm 119 as long as needed. Get an understanding to the point it becomes a lifestyle change. Take a challenge to block excuses, distractions, blame, and routine that attempt to get in the way of obedience. Remember this is to **build relationship not religion**.

DISCRECTION ADVISED

Psalm 120
A song of ascents.

1 I call on the Lord in my distress,
  and he answers me.
2 Save me, Lord,
  from lying lips
  and from deceitful tongues.
3 What will he do to you,
  and what more besides,
  you deceitful tongue?
4 He will punish you with a warrior's sharp arrows,
  with burning coals of the broom bush.
5 Woe to me that I dwell in Meshek,
  that I live among the tents of Kedar!
6 Too long have I lived
  among those who hate peace.
7 I am for peace;
  but when I speak, they are for war.

Anytime you make a decision to elevate higher, or make a change for the better to follow the Lord negative will influences arise. Unknown of the specific psalmist; this Psalm clearly describes extreme anxiety overwhelming the mind. The call for help was heard by the Lord. Lies, manipulation, and deception attempted to attach itself to the character of the psalmist. The environment was so bad it was referred to as a place of darkness (tents of Kadar). Flesh could have easily taken its course and retaliation would have been the first response. Too many times familiarity and feelings have distorted the future (vs.6).

Discretion is critical and must be utilized in the journey from Jezebel (evil spirits) to Justice (Kingdom mentality).

Learning to dust the opinions of man, feelings of acceptance, and the brokenness of past unhealthy relationships out of sight and mind causes one to not only have but maintain peace.

PRAYER

I call on the Voice of Truth today. Forgive me for allowing my feelings to defend me. Today I make a conscious decision to rise above every hater, naysayer, and backbiter in my life. The devil is the father of lies and there is no truth in him (John 8:44). No longer do the lies of my past, present, or future are attached to me. Save me O Lord from lying lips and from deceitful tongues(vs.2). I am not perfect but I serve a God who is! I rise above petty arguments, disagreements, misjudgments, immature attitudes, gossip, drama, competition, jealousy, and envious actions. I choose discretion, peace, and the joy of the Lord as a tool of assassination against the enemy in Jesus name I pray Amen.

NO DAYS OFF

Psalm 121
A song of ascents.

1 I lift up my eyes to the mountains
   where does my help come from?
2 My help comes from the Lord,
   the Maker of heaven and earth.
3 He will not let your foot slip
   he who watches over you will not slumber;
4 indeed, he who watches over Israel
   will neither slumber nor sleep.
5 The Lord watches over you
   the Lord is your shade at your right hand;
6 the sun will not harm you by day,
   nor the moon by night.
7 The Lord will keep you from all harm
   he will watch over your life;
8 the Lord will watch over your coming and going
   both now and forevermore.

Dangers, testing's, and transitions of life will always be among the living. This confident Psalm demands hope in the heart of the reader that the Lord is always with you. Many times we question God and wonder, ponder, and doubt if change will ever happen. Securing your faith in the resolution and not the problem allows help from the Lord to fly freely to the rescue. Day in, day out, not skipping a beat, pausing for a rest, contemplating a thought, or break for vacation is not in His character. His desire is to protect, strengthen, and guide those who lift (exalt, promote, raise, look, desire) their hope to the maker of the heaven and earth.

Pray Psalm 121

GO WHERE THE GLORY IS

Psalm 122
A song of ascents. Of David.

1 I rejoiced with those who said to me,
  "Let us go to the house of the Lord."
2 Our feet are standing
  in your gates, Jerusalem.
3 Jerusalem is built like a city
  that is closely compacted together.
4 That is where the tribes go up
  the tribes of the Lord
  to praise the name of the Lord
  according to the statute given to Israel.
5 There stand the thrones for judgment,
  the thrones of the house of David.
6 Pray for the peace of Jerusalem:
  "May those who love you be secure.
7 May there be peace within your walls
  and security within your citadels."
8 For the sake of my family and friends,
  I will say, "Peace be within you."
9 For the sake of the house of the Lord our God,
  I will seek your prosperity.

Jerusalem was the city that was set apart from everybody else as the very place where God's presence was. David was elated to be a part of what was about to take place. Approaching the house of the Lord was pure and without regard to who will be there, what would I benefit from this, or how long is this going to be. Jerusalem represented stability, peace, prosperity, unity, and beautifully adorned with God's love. This was not a custom nor religion but it was a lifestyle David lived.

Prayer was the incense and seeking the glory was the reward. At the present time the church is a typology of Jerusalem; and we must be like David and rejoice in going where the glory is!

PRAYER

Father you are the King of glory. Your glory is my rear guard (Isaiah 58:8) that provides protection and stability for my life. Let the glory of the Lord rise and let every enemy be scattered (Psalm 68:1). I will enter into the house of the Lord withholding nothing and surrender to Your glory. I will rejoice in your glory now and forevermore in Jesus name I pray Amen.

EYES WIDE OPEN

Psalm 123
A song of ascents.

1 I lift up my eyes to you,
  to you who sit enthroned in heaven.
2 As the eyes of slaves look to the hand of their master,
  as the eyes of a female slave look to the hand of her mistress,
  so our eyes look to the Lord our God,
  till he shows us his mercy.
3 Have mercy on us, Lord, have mercy on us,
  for we have endured no end of contempt.
4 We have endured no end
  of ridicule from the arrogant,
  of contempt from the proud.

Children require much attention from their parents and are very dependent on their care. When hunger strikes, diapers need changing, tummy aches, and tears of pain occur they look to the ones who can give them relief. This Psalm describes how people look inwardly and outwardly to the Lord for His great mercies of relief. I am sure this journey has been difficult and quite restless to deal with socially and emotionally. The attitude and action was to set their eyes face forward to the goal ahead with patience.

When people disrespect you and attempt to discard your name and who you represent; allow faith and patience the upper hand to set your vision on the mercies of the Lord. Their eyes never shifted to the situation but to the solution. Sweet relief is always found in the mercies of God every single day.

PRAYER

I lift up my eyes to You. My natural eyes are set to read the promises of Your word. My spiritual eyes are prepared to believe the supernatural promises of Your word. I look to You for relief and depend on You to help me patiently deal with people and situations that are beyond my control. Help me maintain focus even when frustration attempts to throw me off course. Father you delight in showing your mercy (Micah 7:18). I look to Your mercy for me today in Jesus name I pray Amen.

DECLARED DELIVERANCE

Psalm 124
A song of ascents. Of David.

1 If the Lord had not been on our side
  let Israel say
2 if the Lord had not been on our side
  when people attacked us,
3 they would have swallowed us alive
  when their anger flared against us;
4 the flood would have engulfed us,
  the torrent would have swept over us,
5 the raging waters
  would have swept us away.
6 Praise be to the Lord,
  who has not let us be torn by their teeth.
7 We have escaped like a bird
  from the fowler's snare;
  the snare has been broken,
  and we have escaped.
8 Our help is in the name of the Lord,
  the Maker of heaven and earth.

David and the people of Israel were unified in the Lord's power of protection over them. No matter how deep and ugly the situation was; the testimony of still being alive was credited to the name of the Lord. One step away from the enemy's trap, death literally staring in their faces, continuously reminded of the depletion of personal freedom caused for a celebration of praise. Through it all the Lord was on their side. This Psalm speaks of great appreciation in their deliverance and not taking it for granted. Recognizing the importance of the Lord's presence blesses those who understand that they cannot do it alone.

PRAYER

Blessed be the Lord for my help is in the name of the Lord.

• Had it not been for the Lord who was on my side: I would be a worthless case for it is by the Lord's mercies I am not consumed (Lamentations 3:22)

• Had it not been for the Lord on my side: I would be trapped by my past, unforgiven, and lost. Lord you are a very present help (Psalm 46:1)

• Had it not been for the Lord on my side: I would not be able to have hope for tomorrow, or given a second chance. Your grace is sufficient (2 Corinthians 12:9)

• Had it not been for the Lord on my side: my identity and destiny would be limited to man's opinion. But thanks be unto God who always causes me to triumph (2 Corinthians 2:14)

Lord I know You are fighting for me as I continue to trust You are on my side in Jesus name I pray Amen.

IN GOD WE TRUST

Psalm 125
A song of ascents.

1 Those who trust in the Lord are like Mount Zion,
  which cannot be shaken but endures forever.
2 As the mountains surround Jerusalem,
  so the Lord surrounds his people
  both now and forevermore.
3 The scepter of the wicked will not remain
  over the land allotted to the righteous,
  for then the righteous might use
  their hands to do evil.
4 Lord, do good to those who are good,
  to those who are upright in heart.
5 But those who turn to crooked ways
  the Lord will banish with the evildoers.
  Peace be on Israel.

Trust requires commitment and patience. Trust builds relationship that cannot be distracted by any outside influence. Trust qualifies you with stability to stand and enables you with authority. Trust establishes character and prepares to endure even in the worst of times.

There was no turning back now on this journey. The people of Israel dedicated themselves to God's plan for their life. Temptation attempted to pull them out from their God-given position. Their journey was an emotional roller coaster but God promises to always protect those who put solid trust in Him. The enemy tried to dictate that what God already wrote as victory. Lasting peace was the benefit they obtained by trusting in God.

PRAYER

Trust in the Lord with all thine heart and lean not into their own understanding in all thy ways acknowledge him and he will direct your path (Proverbs 3:5-6). Forgive me for not trusting You at times when life crutched my faith. I trust You will take care of me, for the entrance of your word brings light (Psalm 119:130). This world is full of good and evil but nothing shall separate me from trusting You. In God I trust and I am committed to keeping my mind off idol behaviors and focus on purpose. You said in Your word trust in the Lord and do good (Psalm 37:3). No matter what arises I will remain confident in expectation and I shall not be moved. My relationship with You is built on trust, faith, and love. Thank You for being a shield around me everywhere that I go (Psalm 3:3). In God I trust. Hallelujah in Jesus name I pray Amen.

RESTORE US AGAIN

Psalm 126
A song of ascents.

1 When the Lord restored the fortunes of Zion,
  we were like those who dreamed.
2 Our mouths were filled with laughter,
  our tongues with songs of joy.
  Then it was said among the nations,
  "The Lord has done great things for them."
3 The Lord has done great things for us,
  and we are filled with joy.
4 Restore our fortunes, Lord,
  like streams in the Negev.
5 Those who sow with tears
  will reap with songs of joy.
6 Those who go out weeping,
  carrying seed to sow,
  will return with songs of joy,
  carrying sheaves with them.

Life seems pretty easy when all is going well. We smile, we laugh, and get along with others; then **LIFE** has a funny way of interrupting **LIFE**. No matter how difficult life can be the most important thing is to live it with hope (quote unknown).

The people of Israel encountered countless blessings as a nation and everyone took notice. They did not hold back their gratitude towards God as they remember many dark seasons that occurred. Now they have come to another dry season where not everyone in the community feels that same gratitude anymore. A unified prayer for restoration was started for those who felt depleted, sowing and not receiving harvest, hurting hearts, defeated mentalities, and bruised faith. This was a great resolution with pure intentions that was selflessly done in a way that God can work in and bless. Their testimonies of hope as a nation unified them to prayer that if God has restored us once He will do it again. This is a subtle reminder that we should always testify of the miracles in our lives that no one but God could have restored us from. We must also posture ourselves to pray for our fellow man to have faith to believe and receive it for their lives as well.

PRAYER

As I look back over my life I am filled with joy because of what You have brought me out, through, and from! I now understand those places in my life were not to ridicule me but to refine me on purpose! Every circumstance that held my faith captive is restored 100 fold in my life **NOW**! Your word says those who sow in tears will reap with songs of joy. He who goes out weeping carrying seed to sow will return with songs of joy carrying sheaves with him (vs.5-6). I will not be weary in well doing (Galatians 6:9). Streams of restoration are flowing in my life; all things are working for my good (Romans 8:28). Your grace covers me and I am grateful. I pray also for those who are hurting as I did and asked that You water them with your word (Ephesians 5:26) and restore them. All this newness of life is from God, who brought us back to himself through what Christ did. And God has given us the task of reconciling people to him (2 Corinthians 5:18). May my life reflect the goodness of Your glory to all mankind today, in Jesus name I pray Amen.

UNLESS THE LORD BUILDS

Psalm 127
A song of ascents. Of Solomon.

1 Unless the Lord builds the house,
  the builders labor in vain.
  Unless the Lord watches over the city,
  the guards stand watch in vain.
2 In vain you rise early
  and stay up late,
  toiling for food to eat
  for he grants sleep to those he loves.
3 Children are a heritage from the Lord,
  offspring a reward from him.
4 Like arrows in the hands of a warrior
  are children born in one's youth.
5 Blessed is the man
  whose quiver is full of them.
  They will not be put to shame
  when they contend with their opponents in court.

Here is a two-part Psalm explaining David's wise advice to his son Solomon. God placed supernatural wisdom and wealth in Solomon; but as a natural son he still had to be raised on how to be a godly man. The first part of the Psalm (verses 1-2) separates those who follow instructions, and those who fall prey to the "other" influences. David is teaching him to be very mindful of keeping God first in every area and decision of everyday life. Do not become hotheaded and allow work and other projects (people, business, social media) consume your time that should be spent with God. He assures it is not in seeking to do everything right but dependent on God to make everything right in us.

The second part (verses 3-5) explains advice on building family through the promises of God. As parents we have a responsibility to teach our children the fear and instructions of God's perfect plan. This builds stability and faith in our children. David loved his son and was delighted in sharing the blessings to godly success. He boasted in himself as blessed because he knew his gifts (children) were from God and would be a reflection of His glory.

PRAYER

Unless the Lord builds the house:
I will stand still and wait patiently to hear your instruction

Unless the Lord builds the house:
I will hold my tongue and allow the Holy Spirit to speak for me

Unless the Lord builds the house:
I will not get weary in well doing and I will press forward

Unless the Lord builds the house:
I will teach my children and raise them up to be a godly success even when they are rebellious and irresponsible

Unless the Lord builds the house:
I will not allow time wasters to use my energy or hinder my quiet time with you

Build me up, fill me up, raise me up. Shape, make, and mold me to wholeness. Help me to remain humble and teachable to receive constructive criticism that will strengthen me to be a better me! Unless the Lord builds the house I am just a filthy rag (Isaiah 64:6). Equip me to build in Jesus name I pray Amen.

LIFESTYLE OF THE BLESSED AND OBEDIENT
(GREAT FOR MEN)

Psalm 128
A song of ascents.

1 Blessed are all who fear the Lord,
  who walk in obedience to him.
2 You will eat the fruit of your labor;
  blessings and prosperity will be yours.
3 Your wife will be like a fruitful vine
  within your house;
  your children will be like olive shoots
  around your table.
4 Yes, this will be the blessing
  for the man who fears the Lord.
5 May the Lord bless you from Zion;
  may you see the prosperity of Jerusalem
  all the days of your life.
6 May you live to see your children's children
  peace be on Israel.

This short but instructive Psalm explains how the life of the believer should live. It is important to establish your household according to the ways of the Lord. Blessings on job or business (vs.2), marriage (vs.3), health and children (vs.3), the church you are connected to (vs.5), and your children's children are depended upon your obedience. Dating back to when this Psalm was written to the people of Israel is no different to the generation we now live in today. Walking in fear (respect, honor, instructions) of the Lord gives permission for the blessings to flow as they should in our lives.

The solid foundation of your home spiritually and physically should be lived out loud as a lifestyle for all to be encouraged in and eager to live as well.

PRAYER

How happy are those who fear the Lord all who follow his ways! You will enjoy the fruit of your labor. How happy you will be! How rich your life! Your wife will be like a fruitful vine, flourishing within your home. And look at all those children! There they sit around your table as vigorous and healthy as young olive trees. That is the Lord's reward for those who fear him (vs:1-4).

Psalm 25:14 says… Friendship with the Lord is reserved for those who fear him. With them he shares the secrets of his covenant. Open the eyes of my heart to follow You fully. My prayer is for my marriage, children, family, money, career, church, and health be blessed. I know every day will not be easy nor will I pass every test but I do put my faith in Your word. I will build myself up in holy faith and pray in the spirit (Jude 1:20) to live a life that pleases You. Man can only provide temporary what You provide eternally. Worldly pleasures do not make a house a home. Spiritual submission to Your will makes a home sweet home physically and spiritually (1 John 2:15-17). May the Lord bless me all the days of my life as I walk with Him in spirit and in truth (John 4:24) in Jesus name I pray Amen.

FREE INDEED

Psalm 129
A song of ascents.

1 "They have greatly oppressed me from my youth,"
   let Israel say;
2 "they have greatly oppressed me from my youth,
   but they have not gained the victory over me.
3 Plowmen have plowed my back
   and made their furrows long.
4 But the Lord is righteous;
   he has cut me free from the cords of the wicked."
5 May all who hate Zion
   be turned back in shame.
6 May they be like grass on the roof,
   which withers before it can grow;
7 a reaper cannot fill his hands with it,
   nor one who gathers fill his arms.
8 May those who pass by not say to them,
   "The blessing of the Lord be on you;
   we bless you in the name of the Lord."

One of the secrets of life is to make stepping stones out of stumbling blocks (Jack Penn). There is nothing more peaceful than not just being free but being free **INDEED**!

The difference between the two (M.W defined) is:

> ➢ Free: not under control or in the power of another

> ➢ Indeed: to further emphasize a statement, confirm something already suggested, or introduce a stronger point

The psalmist from a very young age had been confined to the opinions of man's point of view and looked upon as a useless weak statistic that would never amount to anything. The Israelites bashed the writer's self-esteem and crushed their confidence.

It was an everyday battle in the psalmist community, home, and relationships. Through it all the psalmist refused to believe man's report. The psalmist chose to be set free from the attachments of foul spirits, negative influences, dirty dealings, and those who do not believe in godly potential. He began to pray that God would deal with it and make them eat their words. Do not allow your potential and purpose the mediocrity of average. Press for the limitless power in the arms of the Lord to be free INDEED!

PRAYER

Hallelujah! Today marks the day that I am free indeed. Free indeed from the inside out to live the life You have set before me. Your word says…Whom the Son sets free is free indeed (John 8:36). My confidence and self-esteem shall rise and shine through the promises of Your word. I am an overcomer! Free indeed from yesterday's pain and today's sorrows for You are the Lord who goes before me (Deut. 31:8). Free indeed from shame and disrespect. I pay no attention to mediocre messes. I am a child of God! Free indeed; I am fearfully and wonderfully made (Psalm 139:14). You turn my ashes to beauty, sorrow to joy, mourning to dancing, and the spirit of heaviness for a garment of praise (Isaiah 61:3). I follow your lead Holy Spirit. I give myself permission to be free indeed. I call on the Lord and I am helped (Psalm 28:7). Hallelujah in Jesus name I pray Amen.

TIME OUT
(*PENITENTIAL PSALM*)

Psalm 130
A song of ascents.

1 Out of the depths I cry to you, Lord;
2 Lord, hear my voice.
   Let your ears be attentive
   to my cry for mercy.
3 If you, Lord, kept a record of sins,
   Lord, who could stand?
4 But with you there is forgiveness,
   so that we can, with reverence, serve you.
5 I wait for the Lord, my whole being waits,
   and in his word I put my hope.
6 I wait for the Lord
   more than watchmen wait for the morning,
   more than watchmen wait for the morning.
7 Israel, put your hope in the Lord,
   for with the Lord is unfailing love
   and with him is full redemption.
8 He himself will redeem Israel
   from all their sins.

Forgiveness is a privilege that must be taken very seriously. God is the only one who can judge and this mature psalmist understood that total restoration could only be found in Him. The psalmist sins had him so bound in darkness and deep depression the only way out was to look up to the mercies of God. It was enough of living in the cycle of defeat and playing hide and seek; it was time to get serious for God. This wait was not just physical it was a spiritual wait that allowed the mind, soul, and flesh to line up with the spirit to produce total restoration and redemption. Literally in the timeout corner; the psalmist knew personally my life is a mess that needs a miracle!

Twice stated in verse 6 reveals intense hunger of doing whatever it takes to live in the freedom of forgiveness. Forgiveness is not just a choice it is a decision to position oneself in full surrender to wholeness in God.

PRAYER

Pray 131 1- 6:

Out of the depths I cry to you, Lord; Lord, hear my voice.

Let your ears be attentive to my cry for mercy. If you, Lord, kept   a record of sins, Lord, who could stand? But with you there is forgiveness, so that we can, with reverence, serve you. I wait for the Lord, my whole being waits, and in his word I put my hope.

I wait for the Lord more than watchmen wait for the morning, more than watchmen wait for the morning.

Forgive me Father of my wrongs I have done. There is no greater feeling in knowing I am forgiven; Your word says in 1 John 1:9…If we confess our sins, he is faithful and just and will forgive us our sins and purify us from all unrighteousness. I put myself in time out from the distractions that have disturbed me for reaching my dreams and goals of destiny and purpose. Jesus Christ came into the world to save sinners of whom I am the worst (1 Timothy 1:15). Who am I to deserve such a gift that cannot be repaid by mere human efforts. I am an heir and I am forgiven. I have redemption through the blood of Jesus. My submission to Your salvation is all You ask of me and I freely receive Your free gift of grace in Jesus name I pray Amen.

MANAGING SPIRITUAL AUTHOURITY

Psalm 131
A song of ascents. Of David.

1 My heart is not proud, Lord,
  my eyes are not haughty;
  I do not concern myself with great matters
  or things too wonderful for me.
2 But I have calmed and quieted myself,
  I am like a weaned child with its mother;
  like a weaned child I am content.
3 Israel, put your hope in the Lord
  both now and forevermore.

David learned how not to concern himself with people or situations that did not connect with his faith or his purpose. Speaking from his heart he knew what his flesh was capable of but restrained from reacting to it. Growing in the Lord requires much patience and learning how to maintain it with a thankful attitude. Managing emotions became easier for David the more he understood when to disconnect from them and give faith room to grow. Humility and a teachable spirit makes one soul sit still and respect spiritual authority. David deepened his relationship in the Lord by maturing in these areas of his life. He knew it had to be done in him and not others (judging) who he felt needed it more than him. He confirmed through his lifestyle as being the salt; and continued emerging as a leader to all the people of Israel to manage themselves in the same way to win souls for the Lord.

PRAYER

My heart is not proud, Lord, my eyes are not haughty; I do not concern myself with great matters or things too wonderful for me. But I have calmed and quieted myself, I am like a weaned child with its mother; like a weaned child I am content (vs.1-2). Help me Lord to maintain; there is always room for improvement and it begins with me. I set my face like flint (Isaiah 50:7) determined to do Your will. My heart is a tablet (Proverbs 3:3) and my tongue is the pen (Psalm 45:1). I pray to avoid confrontations that bring stress and confusion to my life. I want to grow and learn to make better decisions concerning my faith in You. I will never be able to know everything or pretend to be someone I am not. I submit to Your tough love that redeems me as righteous. I push to model behaviors that lead others to Your love. Today I manage myself with spiritual maturity; I can do all things through Christ who strengthens me (Philippians 4:13) in Jesus name I pray Amen.

DONNA ROBINSON

MAKE ROOM

Psalm 132
A song of ascents.

1 Lord, remember David
  and all his self-denial.
2 He swore an oath to the Lord,
  he made a vow to the Mighty One of Jacob:
3 "I will not enter my house
  or go to my bed,
4 I will allow no sleep to my eyes
  or slumber to my eyelids,
5 till I find a place for the Lord,
  a dwelling for the Mighty One of Jacob."
6 We heard it in Ephrathah,
  we came upon it in the fields of Jaar:
7 "Let us go to his dwelling place,
  let us worship at his footstool, saying,
8 'Arise, Lord, and come to your resting place,
  you and the ark of your might.
9 May your priests be clothed with your righteousness;
  may your faithful people sing for joy.'"
10 For the sake of your servant David,
  do not reject your anointed one.
11 The Lord swore an oath to David,
  a sure oath he will not revoke:
  "One of your own descendants
  I will place on your throne.
12 If your sons keep my covenant
  and the statutes I teach them,
  then their sons will sit
  on your throne for ever and ever."
13 For the Lord has chosen Zion,
  he has desired it for his dwelling, saying,
14 "This is my resting place for ever and ever;
  here I will sit enthroned, for I have desired it.
15 I will bless her with abundant provisions;
  her poor I will satisfy with food.
16 I will clothe her priests with salvation,
  and her faithful people will ever sing for joy.
17 "Here I will make a horn grow for David
  and set up a lamp for my anointed one.

18 I will clothe his enemies with shame,
   but his head will be adorned with a radiant crown."

There is much to be said of this Psalm. I am only led to focus on the main point of this Psalm of ascent. This Psalm teaches the vitality of the presence of the Lord. David endured sleepless nights listening for instructions; and his son is now reminded of them. Samuel was given the responsibility with preparing a place for the presence of the Lord to reside in. Order was now being established by setting aside personal agendas; and this dwelling place had been promised by the Lord to position the people for abundant provision to those who chose to go there and receive it. The lineage of David as King and those who will reign as King after **<u>EVEN</u>** Christ were spoken of as a definite reminder of this covenant; His presence will not be broken. Every believer must continue to vow (commit) and "clothe" (live) themselves to make room for the strength of His presence the Anointed One.

PRAYER

O Lord Your presence is what I need to survive. Without Your presence I cannot function. I listen and quiet my soul day and night to wait for Your instructions to guide me. I pray for my heart to open up for true salvation and make room for Your presence to dwell. I set my mind, movement, and money to be clothed with the satisfaction of Your presence. Let all the other names fade away that cloud my spirit and may the heavens open up over my life and crown me with everlasting joy! I prepare my days ahead with expectation that Your presence is always near and Your Holy Spirit fills me to overflowing in Jesus name I pray Amen.

ANOINTED BY ASSOCIATION

Psalm 133
A song of ascents. Of David.

1 How good and pleasant it is
   when God's people live together in unity!
2 It is like precious oil poured on the head,
   running down on the beard,
   running down on Aaron's beard,
   down on the collar of his robe.
3 It is as if the dew of Hermon
   were falling on Mount Zion.
   For there the Lord bestows his blessing,
   even life forevermore.

Unity was at an all-time high! A celebration to be remembered as David wrote with great joy and excitement of this experience. Something supernatural happens when everyone is on one accord; it cannot be interrupted. The nation of Israel were in agreement at Zion of the Lord's unbreakable covenant promises. It resembled the sacred oil used to anoint Aaron; and the dew that flows from the highest mountain peak upon those who rest in Zion. Through all the battles fought, betrayal, and bitter relationships; David and the Israelites endured this as an experience that blessed them completely. Anointed by association is now available for all mankind through Christ Jesus to experience as the Bible declares in the book of Ephesians. The Lord pours out in blessings that never run dry.

PRAYER

Selflessly lift up this nation to unify under the anointing and grace of God as a force of power against the enemy. Pray 133…

How good and pleasant it is

when God's people live together in unity!

It is like precious oil poured on the head,

running down on the beard,

running down on Aaron's beard,

down on the collar of his robe.

It is as if the dew of Hermon

were falling on Mount Zion.

For there the Lord bestows his blessing,

even life forevermore.

Father today unify:

Churches, leaders, political figures, marriages, educational systems, county leaders, families, global regions, governmental authorities, Pastors, lay members, apostles, Bishops, CEOs, motivational speakers, Authors, Doctors, Lawyers, nonprofit organizations, celebrities, legendary role models, humanitarians, singers, songwriters, Ministers, Elders, Directors in leadership roles, Commissioners, cultures, communities, local authorities, Republicans, Democrats, Independent parties, and the body of Christ to synchronize through the Holy Spirit on one accord that would shake the enemy to his knees (Acts 2). How good and pleasant it is when God's people live together in unity! In Jesus name I pray Amen.

THE BENEDICTION

Psalm 134
A song of ascents.

1 Praise the Lord, all you servants of the Lord
  who minister by night in the house of the Lord.
2 Lift up your hands in the sanctuary
  and praise the Lord.
3 May the Lord bless you from Zion,
  he who is the Maker of heaven and earth.

The journey is coming to a close and church is about to be over. Praise is still going forth for all the Lord has done. The servants of the Lord referred to in this Psalm are the Priests and the Levites. They both play different roles in serving the temple (church). Some of the responsibilities of the Levites are the upkeep of the temple, assist Priests, and stay on guard as watchmen of the sacred objects in the temple. Priests were given the assignment to minister the word of the Lord, live holy and pure. The Israelites were simply blessing them in prayer for the Lord to continue in instructing and strengthening them. The "night" indicates the rough and dark times that their servitude would not grow weary. The Israelites were thankful to the Lord.

PRAYER

I lift my hands to You and praise Your name. I pray You bless my Pastor (name) in strength and wisdom.

I thank You for my Pastor and leading me to (church name). I pray Pastor (name) grow in the grace and knowledge of his or her calling.

Allow his or her heart to continue to live as a servant first and humble in the sight of God and man. I pray over his or her marriage, home, family, finances, and social influence for the perfect will of God to be done. Enlarge his or her vision for supernatural impartation. Download revelation beyond their mental capacity. Give them a prophetic tongue to speak over the lives of Your people. I declare he or she will not grow weary in well doing. Where they are weak You make them strong. I hold up the arms of my Pastor as Aaron did with Moses (Exodus 17:12). I pray a Numbers 6 blessing over them. You said in your word… How beautiful are the feet of those who bring the good news (Romans 10:15) in Jesus name I pray Amen.

REASONS TO PRAISE

Psalm 135

1 Praise the Lord.
  Praise the name of the Lord;
  praise him, you servants of the Lord,
2 you who minister in the house of the Lord,
  in the courts of the house of our God.
3 Praise the Lord, for the Lord is good;
  sing praise to his name, for that is pleasant.
4 For the Lord has chosen Jacob to be his own,
  Israel to be his treasured possession.
5 I know that the Lord is great,
  that our Lord is greater than all gods.
6 The Lord does whatever pleases him,
  in the heavens and on the earth,
  in the seas and all their depths.
7 He makes clouds rise from the ends of the earth;
  he sends lightning with the rain
  and brings out the wind from his storehouses.
8 He struck down the firstborn of Egypt,
  the firstborn of people and animals.
9 He sent his signs and wonders into your midst, Egypt,
  against Pharaoh and all his servants.
10 He struck down many nations
  and killed mighty kings
11 Sihon king of the Amorites,
  Og king of Bashan,
  and all the kings of Canaan
12 and he gave their land as an inheritance,
  an inheritance to his people Israel.
13 Your name, Lord, endures forever,
  your renown, Lord, through all generations.
14 For the Lord will vindicate his people
  and have compassion on his servants.
15 The idols of the nations are silver and gold,
  made by human hands.
16 They have mouths, but cannot speak,
  eyes, but cannot see.
17 They have ears, but cannot hear,
  nor is there breath in their mouths.
18 Those who make them will be like them,

and so will all who trust in them.
19 All you Israelites, praise the Lord;
    house of Aaron, praise the Lord;
20 house of Levi, praise the Lord;
    you who fear him, praise the Lord.
21 Praise be to the Lord from Zion,
    to him who dwells in Jerusalem.
    Praise the Lord.

Recalling much of what has already been said in previous Psalms and books of the Old Testament. This Psalm is not short of praise. The psalmist leads the reader on the historic journey of the Lord's sovereignty at work for His chosen nation of Israel.

Acknowledging the truth of there should never be a moment too dark that cancels the opportunity to give Him praise. Intentionally praising the Lord for who He is and understanding that all creation was designed for this. Warnings are given to not fall victim to false gods which produce false praise. Do not be moved by worldly impersonations that observe praise as unnecessary or uninspiring. Every praise belongs to the **ONE** who is praise and those who dwell in it.

PRAYER

Glory to God I've got a reason and a right to give You praise. I was created to make your praise glorious (Psalm 66:2). I enter into your courts with praise (Psalm 100:4). You have been my way of escape through times I thought I would never make it out of. You breathe new life in my spirit to move forward. Hallelujah, I praise you God and I refuse to let the rocks cry out. Praise is who I am. Praise is what I do. Praise is where You are. All glory, majesty, power and authority belongs to you Lord (Jude 1:25). The Lord is my strength and my defense my salvation he is my God and I will praise him (Exodus 15:2). Breath in my body, clothes on my back, food to eat, a job to go, eyes to see, limbs that move, a voice to speak! I won't hold back my praise! I will sing to the Lord for he has been good to me (Psalms 13:6). You have been faithful and I will tell the world that Your praise will ever be on my lips and continually be in my mouth! In Jesus name I pray Amen.

ALL IN THE NAME OF LOVE

Psalm 136
1 Give thanks to the Lord, for he is good.
  His love endures forever.
2 Give thanks to the God of gods.
  His love endures forever.
3 Give thanks to the Lord of lords:
  His love endures forever.
4 to him who alone does great wonders,
  His love endures forever.
5 who by his understanding made the heavens,
  His love endures forever.
6 who spread out the earth upon the waters,
  His love endures forever.
7 who made the great lights
  His love endures forever.
8 the sun to govern the day,
  His love endures forever.
9 the moon and stars to govern the night;
  His love endures forever.
10 to him who struck down the firstborn of Egypt
  His love endures forever.
11 and brought Israel out from among them
  His love endures forever.
12 with a mighty hand and outstretched arm;
  His love endures forever.
13 to him who divided the Red Sea asunder
  His love endures forever.
14 and brought Israel through the midst of it,
  His love endures forever.
15 but swept Pharaoh and his army into the Red Sea;
  His love endures forever.
16 to him who led his people through the wilderness;
  His love endures forever.
17 to him who struck down great kings,
  His love endures forever.
18 and killed mighty kings
  His love endures forever.
19 Sihon king of the Amorites
  His love endures forever.
20 and Og king of Bashan
  His love endures forever.

21 and gave their land as an inheritance,
   His love endures forever.
22 an inheritance to his servant Israel.
   His love endures forever.
23 He remembered us in our low estate
   His love endures forever.
24 and freed us from our enemies.
   His love endures forever.
25 He gives food to every creature.
   His love endures forever.
26 Give thanks to the God of heaven.
   His love endures forever.

Twenty- six times the truth of His love is expressed in this Psalm. Verses 1-9 commands the agape love from the creator of life, heaven and earth, nature's DNA, skies, moon, stars, and the wisdom in which we live in this very day. Verses 10-22 explains the source of Israel's God and Savior; and the miraculous events that occurred as love conquered all. Verses 23-26 gives us a continuance of His love through the redemption of His Son to those nations who were forgotten and held captive of their freedom. Give thanks to the Lord for He is good His love endures forever!

PRAYER

I challenge you to pray Psalms 136 for today. Write down below 26 reasons you love the Creator of your life. Begin to thank Him for His love that is the same yesterday, today, and forever (Heb. 13:8). There is no pit too deep or sin too disappointing that God's love cannot heal. Love conquers **ALL**!

SUFFERING THROUGH SILENCE

Psalm 137

1 By the rivers of Babylon we sat and wept
  when we remembered Zion.
2 There on the poplars
  we hung our harps,
3 for there our captors asked us for songs,
  our tormentors demanded songs of joy;
  they said, "Sing us one of the songs of Zion!"
4 How can we sing the songs of the Lord
  while in a foreign land?
5 If I forget you, Jerusalem,
  may my right hand forget its skill.
6 May my tongue cling to the roof of my mouth
  if I do not remember you,
  if I do not consider Jerusalem
  my highest joy.
7 Remember, Lord, what the Edomites did
  on the day Jerusalem fell.
  "Tear it down," they cried,
  "tear it down to its foundations!"
8 Daughter Babylon, doomed to destruction,
  happy is the one who repays you
  according to what you have done to us.
9 Happy is the one who seizes your infants
  and dashes them against the rocks.

Zion (some translations read Jerusalem) had been ransacked and raided by the Edomite's (remember the "ites") from Babylon. The nation of Israel had done nothing to deserve this treatment being robbed and humiliated in their own community. Held as captives spiritually, physically, and mentally it felt as if God had left them. Battling with thoughts of depression one day, to thoughts of renouncing their religion the next, persuaded to put a pause on praise were easy options.

I am sure we all can relate to this Psalm and learn how to endure with patience (fruit of the spirit) when in reality you really want to exit. By the end of the Psalm it takes a turn and begins to speak the retaliation of God's word over the "ites". These "ites" had struck them where it hurt the most; but prayer and faith was the weapon of choice used to suffer through the silence.

PRAYER

Lord it has been many times I wanted to give up but I hold on to the fruit of patience and endurance to not go at this alone. I know that You are for me. Forgive me for not giving You 100% when I should have. The "ites" in my life are only temporal and today I choose faith and prayer to eliminate the negative. Vengeance is yours Lord (Romans 12:19). I set my mind and keep it set on the plans You have for me and my expected end (Jer. 29:11). The fruits of the spirit (Gal. 5:22-23) will keep me grounded:

Patience will produce perseverance

Peace will set my mind at ease

Self-control will rule over my flesh

Joy will fill my heart

Kindness will witness to others

Love will cover me

Goodness will make me smile

Faithfulness will guide me

Gentleness will soften my attitude

In Jesus name I pray Amen.

BOLD, BRAVE, BLESSED

Psalm 138
Of David.

1 I will praise you, Lord, with all my heart;
   before the "gods" I will sing your praise.
2 I will bow down toward your holy temple
   and will praise your name
   for your unfailing love and your faithfulness,
   for you have so exalted your solemn decree
   that it surpasses your fame.
3 When I called, you answered me;
   you greatly emboldened me.
4 May all the kings of the earth praise you, Lord,
   when they hear what you have decreed.
5 May they sing of the ways of the Lord,
   for the glory of the Lord is great.
6 Though the Lord is exalted, he looks kindly on the lowly;
   though lofty, he sees them from afar.
7 Though I walk in the midst of trouble,
   you preserve my life.
   You stretch out your hand against the anger of my foes;
   with your right hand you save me.
8 The Lord will vindicate me;
   your love, Lord, endures forever
   do not abandon the works of your hands.

I would rather walk with God in the dark than go alone in the light (Mary Gardiner Brainard). Actions and expressions of boasting in God's love gives every believer a right and a reason to have joy. David took authority in his faith and pushed past the distance of natural abilities. Pursuing with passion as a leader, a role model, a man of faith, prayer warrior, and a worshiper. He was determined to live out God's plan for his life. He knew God had placed assignments in him to do and not sit around and procrastinate; but to be proactive and finish them. He did not get all the details in the beginning; he acquired them **along the way**. God's love and loyalty meets at every step. His faithfulness strengthened David when he was weak. This confidence David had in God focused on endurance and not excuses, the positive not the negative, the finish line and not just the starting point! He was bold, brave, and blessed.

PRAYER

Pray Psalms 138

INTENSE INTIMACY

Psalm 139
For the director of music. Of David. A psalm.

1 You have searched me, Lord,
    and you know me.
2 You know when I sit and when I rise;
    you perceive my thoughts from afar.
3 You discern my going out and my lying down;
    you are familiar with all my ways.
4 Before a word is on my tongue
    you, Lord, know it completely.
5 You hem me in behind and before,
    and you lay your hand upon me.
6 Such knowledge is too wonderful for me,
    too lofty for me to attain.
7 Where can I go from your Spirit?
    Where can I flee from your presence?
8 If I go up to the heavens, you are there;
    if I make my bed in the depths, you are there.
9 If I rise on the wings of the dawn,
    if I settle on the far side of the sea,
10 even there your hand will guide me,
    your right hand will hold me fast.
11 If I say, "Surely the darkness will hide me
    and the light become night around me,"
12 even the darkness will not be dark to you;
    the night will shine like the day,
    for darkness is as light to you.
13 For you created my inmost being;
    you knit me together in my mother's womb.
14 I praise you because I am fearfully and wonderfully made;
    your works are wonderful,
    I know that full well.
15 My frame was not hidden from you
    when I was made in the secret place,
    when I was woven together in the depths of the earth.
16 Your eyes saw my unformed body;
    all the days ordained for me were written in your book
    before one of them came to be.
17 How precious to me are your thoughts, God!
    How vast is the sum of them!

18 Were I to count them,
   they would outnumber the grains of sand
   when I awake, I am still with you.
19 If only you, God, would slay the wicked!
   Away from me, you who are bloodthirsty!
20 They speak of you with evil intent;
   your adversaries misuse your name.
21 Do I not hate those who hate you, Lord,
   and abhor those who are in rebellion against you?
22 I have nothing but hatred for them;
   I count them my enemies.
23 Search me, God, and know my heart;
   test me and know my anxious thoughts.
24 See if there is any offensive way in me,
   and lead me in the way everlasting.

The largest room you have is room for improvement (Dr. Mike Freeman). Another up close and personal Psalm of David as another favorite of mine which reveals why he is a man after God's heart (Acts 13:22). Plainly spoken with a strong conviction that his existence is in the God who created him. Uninterrupted from what is seen and heard in the past, present, or future; true purpose is found in God alone.

David was not the perfect or ideal man: family background was dysfunctional, born in sin, most of his decisions in life cost him to battle with depression, adulterer, murderer, fornicator, rejected at a young age, belittled as an adult and father. Through all that God still called him chosen, fearfully and wonderfully made, a thought considered as His child, King, Visionary, giant slayer, servant, obedient and willing, leader, and kingdom survivor. Closely concentrating on himself and asking to be changed of his weak and impure thoughts, actions, and mentalities that minimizes his witness to others.

The omniscient (all knowing) and omnipresence (everywhere at all times) of God never lift from those who have the gift of life and breath in their body.

There is no place too distant in one's life that can hide from the perfect salvation found in the arms of God. A prayer of complete submission and surrender is displayed in this Psalm that leads to everlasting life.

PRAYER

Pray Psalms 139

FREEDOM FIGHTERS

Psalm 140
For the director of music. A psalm of David.

1 Rescue me, Lord, from evildoers;
  protect me from the violent,
2 who devise evil plans in their hearts
  and stir up war every day.
3 They make their tongues as sharp as a serpent's;
  the poison of vipers is on their lips.
4 Keep me safe, Lord, from the hands of the wicked;
  protect me from the violent,
  who devise ways to trip my feet.
5 The arrogant have hidden a snare for me;
  they have spread out the cords of their net
  and have set traps for me along my path.
6 I say to the Lord, "You are my God."
  Hear, Lord, my cry for mercy.
7 Sovereign Lord, my strong deliverer,
  you shield my head in the day of battle.
8 Do not grant the wicked their desires, Lord;
  do not let their plans succeed.
9 Those who surround me proudly rear their heads;
  may the mischief of their lips engulf them.
10 May burning coals fall on them;
  may they be thrown into the fire,
  into miry pits, never to rise.
11 May slanderers not be established in the land;
  may disaster hunt down the violent.
12 I know that the Lord secures justice for the poor
  and upholds the cause of the needy.
13 Surely the righteous will praise your name,
  and the upright will live in your presence.

Standing up for what you believe as a Christian will always bring criticism, threats, and a very small support system. Human nature is more flexible to be swooned by man because their roots are not grounded in fertile soil (belief).

The spirit nature is firm and settled in the truth and freedom of the word of God having the ability to walk in authority. The battles in David's life against King Saul, his son Absalom, the "ites", death threats, and wars reminded him of the Lord's hand of protection on his life. The spirit of David took over human nature and brought release to the outcome of his battles.

As a leader common symptoms of: disrespect, haters, side eye fronts, conflicting conversations, underhanded schemes, haughty attitudes, intimidating personalities, and freeloaders will surface. Obtaining his freedom as a leader came with a fight through much prayer and humility. Fixing his eyes on the security of the Lord allowed the grip of his enemies to release him to freedom.

PRAYER

Rescue me, keep me, and shield me as I fight for my freedom. I have a believer's authority to stand on the head of the enemy. The grip of criticism, slander, bad blood, and immoral actions are released now through the blood of Jesus. Lord be pleased with me for my enemies do not triumph over me (Psalms 41:11). Every hidden snake, trap, plot, and plan have been uprooted from my life. Surely I will praise your name and live upright before you (vs.13). What use to hurt me has been lifted off of me. I will rise in faith as a freedom fighter for my Lord. In Jesus name I pray Amen.

EVERYTHING TO THE LORD IN PRAYER

Psalm 141
A psalm of David.

1 I call to you, Lord, come quickly to me;
   hear me when I call to you.
2 May my prayer be set before you like incense;
   may the lifting up of my hands be like the evening sacrifice.
3 Set a guard over my mouth, Lord;
   keep watch over the door of my lips.
4 Do not let my heart be drawn to what is evil
   so that I take part in wicked deeds
   along with those who are evildoers;
   do not let me eat their delicacies.
5 Let a righteous man strike me that is a kindness;
   let him rebuke me that is oil on my head.
   My head will not refuse it,
   for my prayer will still be against the deeds of evildoers.
6 Their rulers will be thrown down from the cliffs,
   and the wicked will learn that my words were well spoken.
7 They will say, "As one plows and breaks up the earth,
   so our bones have been scattered at the mouth of the grave."
8 But my eyes are fixed on you, Sovereign Lord;
   in you I take refuge do not give me over to death.
9 Keep me safe from the traps set by evildoers,
   from the snares they have laid for me.
10 Let the wicked fall into their own nets,
   while I pass by in safety.

The pressure of retaliation was strong enough to not even consider the consequences at this point! Temptation to follow feelings will lead to confusion and heartbreak. It took all the faith in David to turn the other cheek in this Psalm of prayer. He asked to be heard and be given perfect instructions on how to handle himself. The need to restrain from foul speech and conversations that will cause him to feel a certain type of way.

Most importantly David asked to be lead with tough love, correction, and constructive criticism. This is a mature way to handle arguments and disagreements we have no business troubling ourselves with.

David was treated so unfairly; no one wanted to even listen to him or give him the benefit of the doubt. David was constant in prayer and fixed his eyes in surrender to God. The outstretched arms of the sovereign God are always available quickly to catch us in the net of safety where we are unharmed.

PRAYER

Pray Psalms 141

DESTINY IN THE DARK

Psalm 142
A maskil of David. When he was in the cave. A prayer.

1 I cry aloud to the Lord;
  I lift up my voice to the Lord for mercy.
2 I pour out before him my complaint;
  before him I tell my trouble.
3 When my spirit grows faint within me,
  it is you who watch over my way.
  In the path where I walk
  people have hidden a snare for me.
4 Look and see, there is no one at my right hand;
  no one is concerned for me.
  I have no refuge;
  no one cares for my life.
5 I cry to you, Lord;
  I say, "You are my refuge,
  my portion in the land of the living."
6 Listen to my cry,
  for I am in desperate need;
  rescue me from those who pursue me,
  for they are too strong for me.
7 Set me free from my prison,
  that I may praise your name.
  Then the righteous will gather about me
  because of your goodness to me.

Prostrating yourself in prayer more than your problems releases the power of God to set you free. Although cave complications never seem to go away; prayer will always be **THE** answer to soften the struggles. David refused to be defined by the feelings of defeat. Destiny comes with complications in order to build character. Clearly unaffected by not being accepted with people gave David the spark he needed to move forward.

In this cave of: depression, desperation, anger, limited movement, fear, loneliness, and open wounds is where he found God. Pressing through pain required much faith for the promises to come to pass in his life. David found protection even while in prison spiritually (mind) and physically (cave). Fully unrestricted to go for broke in the spirit; David gave total control over to the Rock of Refuge.

PRAYER

Listen to my cry this day as I pray. When feelings of sadness, anger, grief, low self-esteem, and regret overwhelm my mind **<u>GIVE ME PEACE</u>**. Peace in knowing that I am not alone. Peace in moving forward to the solution. Peace giving me a sound mind to think clear. Help me to grow in my faith and understand my destiny. My acceptance and identity is not based on what people think I am or what problems come my way. I am predestined to win. I am premade with purpose. I am made in Your image. Prayer is designed to access heaven on earth, to shift atmospheres, defeat demons, heal hurt, loose shackles, and move mountains. Let **THIS** prayer remove the darkness from my mind and release light to see again. Greater is He who lives in me (1 John 4:4). I am not controlled by my feelings but in control of my destiny through power, love, and a sound mind. In Jesus name I pray Amen.

DONNA ROBINSON

BREAKING POINT
(*PENITENTIAL PSALM*)

Psalm 143
A psalm of David.

1 Lord, hear my prayer,
   listen to my cry for mercy;
   in your faithfulness and righteousness
   come to my relief.
2 Do not bring your servant into judgment,
   for no one living is righteous before you.
3 The enemy pursues me,
   he crushes me to the ground;
   he makes me dwell in the darkness
   like those long dead.
4 So my spirit grows faint within me;
   my heart within me is dismayed.
5 I remember the days of long ago;
   I meditate on all your works
   and consider what your hands have done.
6 I spread out my hands to you;
   I thirst for you like a parched land.
7 Answer me quickly, Lord;
   my spirit fails.
   Do not hide your face from me
   or I will be like those who go down to the pit.
8 Let the morning bring me word of your unfailing love,
   for I have put my trust in you.
   Show me the way I should go,
   for to you I entrust my life.
9 Rescue me from my enemies, Lord,
   for I hide myself in you.
10 Teach me to do your will,
   for you are my God;
   may your good Spirit
   lead me on level ground.
11 For your name's sake, Lord, preserve my life;
   in your righteousness, bring me out of trouble.
12 In your unfailing love, silence my enemies;
   destroy all my foes,
   for I am your servant.

Breaking point is an experience every human being will encounter in their life. A breaking point is defined as: the point at which a person gives way under stress; the point at which a situation becomes critical; the point at which something loses force or validity (M.W. definition). David finds himself slowly dying from the inside (soul) to be free from petty, unorganized, controlling people. Desiring to hear the voice of God and determined in prayer; David was able to keep his head above water. Reaching this season in his life a choice had to be made to either follow his finicky feelings or make a devoted decision.

The righteousness of God preserves us to keep living. David was damaged goods seeking the faithfulness of God for support. His flesh craved to dictate and weaken him to give up; but deep down in his heart David remembered who he served! Reminded of the Lord's keeping power inspired his courage from being crushed. Sometimes in life the hand that we are dealt seems unbearable to play; but if we study the art of the game (prayer) we can become a **GAME CHANGER**!!

PRAYER

Pray Psalm 143

THE BODYGUARD

Psalm 144
Of David.

1 Praise be to the Lord my Rock,
   who trains my hands for war,
   my fingers for battle.
2 He is my loving God and my fortress,
   my stronghold and my deliverer,
   my shield, in whom I take refuge,
   who subdues peoples under me.
3 Lord, what are human beings that you care for them,
   mere mortals that you think of them?
4 They are like a breath;
   their days are like a fleeting shadow.
5 Part your heavens, Lord, and come down;
   touch the mountains, so that they smoke.
6 Send forth lightning and scatter the enemy;
   shoot your arrows and rout them.
7 Reach down your hand from on high;
   deliver me and rescue me
   from the mighty waters,
   from the hands of foreigners
8 whose mouths are full of lies,
   whose right hands are deceitful.
9 I will sing a new song to you, my God;
   on the ten-stringed lyre I will make music to you,
10 to the One who gives victory to kings,
   who delivers his servant David.
   From the deadly sword
11 Deliver me; and rescue me from the hands
   of foreigners whose mouths are full of lies,
   whose right hands are deceitful.
12 Then our sons in their youth
   will be like well-nurtured plants,
   and our daughters will be like pillars
   carved to adorn a palace.
13 Our barns will be filled
   with every kind of provision.
   Our sheep will increase by thousands,
   by tens of thousands in our fields;
14 our oxen will draw heavy loads.

> There will be no breaching of walls,
> no going into captivity,
> no cry of distress in our streets.
> 15 Blessed is the people of whom this is true;
> blessed is the people whose God is the Lord.

A bodyguard carries an instinct to protect from danger, accompany at all times, and lead with command to move forward. Bodyguards relive one from having to worry and places complete trust of living life unharmed. David pondered who am I (or man) to deserve such special attention. He was humbled personally to God; and valued the commitment of this relationship. Partnering with the unmatched power of God's authority made David a reputable resemblance of authentic servanthood. This triggered all of his enemies to react in complete confusion. Uncompromising his Christianity; he fixed his praise to be new and fresh every day; and the wisdom to remain mindful of his actions. David did not want to stain or taint God's name so he vowed to stay committed as an example in these areas of life:

- A legacy for his children

- A leader to the people

- A living witness of the blessings of the Lord

PRAYER

My shield, my song, and my exceeding great reward. You cover me and lead me safely as I walk this journey.

You are my deliverer and stronghold in times of trouble. Psalms 140:4 says... Keep me, O Lord, from the hands of the wicked; protect me from men of violence who plan to trip my feet. My relationship with You is more important than anybody or anything. Help me to stay "saved". Deliver me from past mistakes, stretch out in me and train my hands for war. O Lord, what is man that you care for him, the son of man that you think of him? Man is like a breath; his days are like a fleeting shadow (vs. 3-4). You know my end from my beginning. You know everything about me, nothing is hidden from You. Take my life, I abandon myself in You. I want to be a living witness of Your righteous right hand. Use me and guide me in glory that testifies of Your love. Protect me from all harm. In Jesus name I pray Amen.

BEYOND THE CALL OF DUTY

Psalm 145
A psalm of praise. Of David.

1 I will exalt you, my God the King;
   I will praise your name for ever and ever.
2 Every day I will praise you
   and extol your name for ever and ever.
3 Great is the Lord and most worthy of praise;
   his greatness no one can fathom.
4 One generation commends your works to another;
   they tell of your mighty acts.
5 They speak of the glorious splendor of your majesty
   and I will meditate on your wonderful works.
6 They tell of the power of your awesome works
   and I will proclaim your great deeds.
7 They celebrate your abundant goodness
   and joyfully sing of your righteousness.
8 The Lord is gracious and compassionate,
   slow to anger and rich in love.
9 The Lord is good to all;
   he has compassion on all he has made.
10 All your works praise you, Lord;
   your faithful people extol you.
11 They tell of the glory of your kingdom
   and speak of your might,
12 so that all people may know of your mighty acts
   and the glorious splendor of your kingdom.
13 Your kingdom is an everlasting kingdom,
   and your dominion endures through all generations.
   The Lord is trustworthy in all he promises
   and faithful in all he does.
14 The Lord upholds all who fall
   and lifts up all who are bowed down.
15 The eyes of all look to you,
   and you give them their food at the proper time.
16 You open your hand
   and satisfy the desires of every living thing.
17 The Lord is righteous in all his ways
   and faithful in all he does.
18 The Lord is near to all who call on him,
   to all who call on him in truth.

19 He fulfills the desires of those who fear him;
   he hears their cry and saves them.
20 The Lord watches over all who love him,
   but all the wicked he will destroy.
21 My mouth will speak in praise of the Lord.
   Let every creature praise his holy name
   for ever and ever.

Overly possessive in his praise, David brags on his God. He details not only about who God is; but what His kingdom represents. David spoke these words from his heart as someone who has experienced having nothing but having everything in God. This praise goes beyond the average clapping of hands. This praise represents the hungry, thirsty, desperate, radical, sincere, serious, foot stomping, war crying, soaked in tears, prostrate flat on the floor type of praise!

This praise crosses over from one generation to the next, it fulfills the desires of every cry, reigns with compassion, and is full of love. David describes God's character which is not complicated, His works that cannot be duplicated, and the greatness of His name that is built to last. David made a clarion call for **ALL** men everywhere to go above and beyond to praise His name forever.

PRAYER

I make a boast in great praise for a great God! Exceedingly, abundantly above all that I could ever imagine (Eph. 3:20) are the works of Your hands. Your kingdom has no end (Luke 1:33 & Isa.9:7) and the glory of the Lord shines on me.

My praise goes beyond all natural limitations and feelings. My praise sets the atmosphere of my day and I say that it shall be great! My praise will satisfy the ear of the Lord and be heard. My praise will embrace the love of His faithfulness towards me! My praise will enlarge my territory and give me vision for my future. My praise will lift up the name of the Lord that endures with all power. The Lord is gracious and compassionate, slow to anger and rich in love. The Lord is good to all; he has compassion on all he has made (vs. 8-9). Your kingdom is an everlasting kingdom and Your dominion endures through all generations. The Lord is faithful to all His promises and loving toward all He has made. The Lord upholds all those who fall and lifts up all who are bowed down. (vs. 13-14). Praise the name of the Lord my God and Savior in Jesus name I pray Amen.

THE BENEFITS OF TRUST

Psalm 146

1 Praise the Lord.
  Praise the Lord, my soul.
2 I will praise the Lord all my life;
  I will sing praise to my God as long as I live.
3 Do not put your trust in princes,
  in human beings, who cannot save.
4 When their spirit departs, they return to the ground;
  on that very day their plans come to nothing.
5 Blessed are those whose help is the God of Jacob,
  whose hope is in the Lord their God.
6 He is the Maker of heaven and earth,
  the sea, and everything in them
  he remains faithful forever.
7 He upholds the cause of the oppressed
  and gives food to the hungry.
  The Lord sets prisoners free,
8 The Lord gives sight to the blind,
  the Lord lifts up those who are bowed down,
  the Lord loves the righteous.
9 The Lord watches over the foreigner
  and sustains the fatherless and the widow,
  but he frustrates the ways of the wicked.
10 The Lord reigns forever,
  your God, O Zion, for all generations.
  Praise the Lord.

Trust is a critical key point to access the kingdom on earth. Trust is the foundation that builds hope in the life of every believer. Trust is not defined by background, upbringing, past, or feelings. Trusting in the Lord challenges the flesh to submit to faith that defies all fears.

The benefits of trust:

• Wholeness and life fulfillment (vs.2)

• Preserved blessings (vs.5&9)

• Relentless faith (vs.6)

• Mind of peace (vs.7)

• Favor (vs.7)

• Vision and creativity (vs.8)

• Real love (vs.8)

• Honest relationships (vs.8)

• New Covenant (vs.9)

God is not like people where trust must be earned. We must trust God with our life, not others viewpoint or reasoning. God confidently offers forgiveness immediately to trust because He desires relationship with the believer. Placing full trust in God will never fall short of strength. Trust repeatedly takes charge to defend the innocent and obedient.

PRAYER

Pray Psalm 146

SUSTAINED WITH SUBSTANCE

Psalm 147
1 Praise the Lord.
   How good it is to sing praises to our God,
   how pleasant and fitting to praise him!
2 The Lord builds up Jerusalem;
   he gathers the exiles of Israel.
3 He heals the brokenhearted
   and binds up their wounds.
4 He determines the number of the stars
   and calls them each by name.
5 Great is our Lord and mighty in power;
   his understanding has no limit.
6 The Lord sustains the humble
   but casts the wicked to the ground.
7 Sing to the Lord with grateful praise;
   make music to our God on the harp.
8 He covers the sky with clouds;
   he supplies the earth with rain
   and makes grass grow on the hills.
9 He provides food for the cattle
   and for the young ravens when they call.
10 His pleasure is not in the strength of the horse,
   nor his delight in the legs of the warrior;
11 the Lord delights in those who fear him,
   who put their hope in his unfailing love.
12 Extol the Lord, Jerusalem;
   praise your God, Zion.
13 He strengthens the bars of your gates
   and blesses your people within you.
14 He grants peace to your borders
   and satisfies you with the finest of wheat.
15 He sends his command to the earth;
   his word runs swiftly.
16 He spreads the snow like wool
   and scatters the frost like ashes.
17 He hurls down his hail like pebbles.
   Who can withstand his icy blast?
18 He sends his word and melts them;
   he stirs up his breezes, and the waters flow.
19 He has revealed his word to Jacob,
   his laws and decrees to Israel.

20 He has done this for no other nation;
    they do not know his laws.
    Praise the Lord.

Everything the Lord has made and all of the capabilities (power) He holds have the power to produce. This causes a chain reaction that releases manifestation (evidence) from heaven to earth. Earth (mankind, believers) is needed to respond to this release through the substance of faith. He cannot work in situations or fix people where He is not wanted, feared, appreciated, or respected. It does not matter how many degrees one may have, outward appearance, number of kind efforts performed, IQ ability, credit score, background, book knowledge, talents, or any other natural abilities that can outdo faith in God's word.

Praise colliding with hope in the Lord produces the substance of faith. Faith then allows the word of God to immediately proceed with action. This Psalm gives the reader firm truths of cause and effect when one sustains their faith in Him. In that time, it was only revealed to the Israelites; but now through Christ Jesus we **ALL** have the privilege in experiencing faith that produces the power of God in our everyday lives.

PRAYER

Praise the Lord. How good it is to sing praises to our God, how pleasant and fitting to praise him (vs.1)! Hebrews 11:1 says... Now faith is being sure of what we hope for and certain of what we do not see.

I believe my faith has been increased because I now understand it outlasts any situation. You have given every man a measure of faith (Rom. 12:3).

I pray the measure I have: heal what is hurting, supply my needs, strengthen me to move forward, position me to pray, defeat my issues, protect me from danger, give me an ear to hear your voice, and bless me with peace. Your word never changes and goes to work on my behalf when I speak in faith. I am sustained with strength. I am consumed in comfort. I am graced in glory. I am prospered in peace as my faith is in You. In Jesus name I pray Amen.

PRAISE IS PRIORITY

Psalm 148

1 Praise the Lord.
  Praise the Lord from the heavens;
  praise him in the heights above.
2 Praise him, all his angels;
  praise him, all his heavenly hosts.
3 Praise him, sun and moon;
  praise him, all you shining stars.
4 Praise him, you highest heavens
  and you waters above the skies.
5 Let them praise the name of the Lord,
  for at his command they were created,
6 and he established them for ever and ever
  he issued a decree that will never pass away.
7 Praise the Lord from the earth,
  you great sea creatures and all ocean depths,
8 lightning and hail, snow and clouds,
  stormy winds that do his bidding,
9 you mountains and all hills,
  fruit trees and all cedars,
10 wild animals and all cattle,
  small creatures and flying birds,
11 kings of the earth and all nations,
  you princes and all rulers on earth,
12 young men and women,
  old men and children.
13 Let them praise the name of the Lord,
  for his name alone is exalted;
  his splendor is above the earth and the heavens.
14 And he has raised up for his people a horn,
  the praise of all his faithful servants,
  of Israel, the people close to his heart.
  Praise the Lord.

Everything the Lord created is commanded to give praise to its' creator. From the heavens to the skies, all creatures and creation, angels, all nations, young and old, to the depths of the sea, and the earth below were made to praise. Expectant praise through His Only Son is prophesied as strength (vs.14 horn) to **ALL** His children.

Priority is only given to what is important. This Psalm encourages praise as the lifeline connection to the Lord. As I write this the city of Orlando mourns the death of 49 lives taken by a terrorist leaving a great number of family members, friends, and co-workers grieving. This is a sincere reminder that the Lord is still worthy of praise even in the midst of unnecessary violent persecution.

Just because a storm comes does not give permission for the trees to just die and the waters to dry up. Even as animals are looked upon as prey does not stop them from being the animal it was created to be! No one and nothing is excluded from giving Him praise. The Lord is in control; He has set everything in its' rightful position to advance through praise.

PRAYER

PRAISE THE LORD! From the rising of the sun to the going down of the same (Psalm 113:3) my lips shall give You praise! I don't wait on the good times to praise, I praise at all times because You are faithful to me! PRAISE THE LORD! My praise allows me to stand in hard times. Praise gives me spiritual authority to silence sadness. PRAISE THE LORD! I have life through my praise, I have joy through my praise, I have peace through my praise! PRAISE THE LORD!

When trials of life come my way I will praise. When people mistreat me I will praise. When I am being tested I will praise. I will be an example of what praise looks like so that others will pledge their praise to the Father who is worthy of it **ALL**. In Jesus name I **PRAY** and **PRAISE** Amen.

PRAISE PARTY

Psalm 149

1 Praise the Lord.
  Sing to the Lord a new song,
  his praise in the assembly of his faithful people.
2 Let Israel rejoice in their Maker;
  let the people of Zion be glad in their King.
3 Let them praise his name with dancing
  and make music to him with timbrel and harp.
4 For the Lord takes delight in his people;
  he crowns the humble with victory.
5 Let his faithful people rejoice in this honor
  and sing for joy on their beds.
6 May the praise of God be in their mouths
  and a double-edged sword in their hands,
7 to inflict vengeance on the nations
  and punishment on the peoples,
8 to bind their kings with fetters,
  their nobles with shackles of iron,
9 to carry out the sentence written against them
  this is the glory of all his faithful people.
  Praise the Lord.

Grateful for the creator. Generous of praise to the Lord. Growing in strength was the response of the children of Israel. The revelation of this Psalm reveals the importance of praise, why it blesses us, and what the Lord does for us through praise. A huge battle against the nation had just been won so they unified and put together the biggest block (praise) party of the year!

Have you ever had a moment in your life when there were no resources, strength, or tears left **BUT GOD** brought you through just in time! The Lord takes delight, enjoyment, and pleasure in us when praise precedes our problems. Now that we are in a time of grace: whenever (vs. 1 new song), wherever (vs.5 bed), and however (vs.3 music/dancing/instruments) He deserves ALL praise!

*I ENCOURAGE YOU TODAY TO LIFT UP YOUR FAITH IN HIM WHO IS ABLE TO DO EXCEEDINGLY (EPH. 3:20)! GO TURN ON SOME ANNOINTED PRAISE MUSIC TO KEEP YOUR SPIRIT LIFTED AND DANCE LIKE NO ONE IS WATCHING!

No prayer today **IT'S ALL PRAISE**!

➢ Take a moment every time you feel blessed give Him praise
➢ Put your car, work, or community radio on a Christian station today
➢ Play some old gospel music or simply sing them yourself
➢ If you have a musical talent use this time to play to the Lord in a song

Let praise be your weapon today!

LET THE BAND PLAY

Psalm 150

1 Praise the Lord.
  Praise God in his sanctuary;
  praise him in his mighty heavens.
2 Praise him for his acts of power;
  praise him for his surpassing greatness.
3 Praise him with the sounding of the trumpet,
  praise him with the harp and lyre,
4 praise him with timbrel and dancing,
  praise him with the strings and pipe,
5 praise him with the clash of cymbals,
  praise him with resounding cymbals.
6 Let everything that has breath praise the Lord.
  Praise the Lord.

The core, the heartbeat, the nucleus, the womb, the definition of what Psalms is all about in this last chapter. Amidst the evil and troubles of injustice, poverty, sickness, and faithlessness there is a sound that must be heard. Our mouths were not just created to eat or voice our opinion; its' main purpose is to PRAISE! The declaration let everything that has breath praise the Lord (vs.6) makes it clear. Let's not deprive our Creator the love and adoration He deserves. This sound is so critical it even has the power to affect our emotions.

As a lover of many genres of music it is so good to understand the sound that expresses emotion from the soul can either stir your spirit or feed your flesh. A solid balance of musical instruments can offer personal motives that please the flesh or offer praise to God. We **ALL** have been given the free will to decide which one to connect with.

Now don't get me wrong I love the 70s, 80s, 90s to now music and the creative artists that have shared their talents with the world; but nothing compares to the praise that should be on **OUR** lips with a drum heartbeat that is lifted towards Him! Our praise combined with a sound of musical rhythms capture heavens attention and sends a wave of restoration to EVERYTHING that has breath.

PRAYER

I want to close this devotional series with a prayer for YOU!

I pray the power of God be released in your life like never before. May the peace of God comfort every area of your life. Let the righteousness of God surround you to defeat every attack in your life. I pray God will pour out His wisdom upon you to walk out your purpose. May God keep a fire lit up under your feet and speak life. I pray the promises of God prosper you in your health physically to serve in the body of Christ. I pray the blood of Jesus from the top of your head to the soles of your feet for complete protection. May your finances flourish from seed to harvest. I pray that your faith will not fail and the word of God dwell richly within you! Signs, miracles, and wonders shall be your portion in Jesus name I pray AMEN!

TERMS/REFERENCES:

- Penitential Psalm: expresses sorrow and the need of forgiveness of sin

- Maskil: understanding, learned, enlightened, to teach

- Song of Ascents: Sang by the people of Israel on their journey to Jerusalem

- Hallelujah Psalms: Hallelujah Psalms begin and end with Praise the Lord or Hallelujah

BACKGROUND

- Solomon: one of David's sons, wisest man ever lived, reigned as King after his father David

REFERENCES:

All scriptures are taken from www.biblegateway.com NIV version

ABOUT THE AUTHOUR

Donna Robinson is a woman of God who possesses a heart of a worshipper. She stands alongside her husband and fully supports him and the vision of New Day Christian Center in Apopka, FL. God has placed unique gifts of discernment, intercession, encourager, and strong leadership qualities in her that will enhance the body of Christ. Native born Floridian she enjoys traveling, music, and lots of shopping! She is a graduate of Valencia Community College with an Associate's Degree in Office Administration and has also obtained her Bachelor's Degree from Barry University in Business Administration with at Specialization in Human Resources. As a mother, wife, friend, and sister she strives to live life as a servant of God.